YO-CAX-668

AUSTRALIAN PARABLES

JOHN PFITZNER

MT. ST. BERNARD COLLEGE
252
PP.
LIBRARY
HERBERTON

Lutheran Publishing House

Copyright © 1988 Lutheran Publishing House.
Except for brief quotations embodied in critical articles and reviews, this book may not
be reproduced in whole or in part by any means whatever without the prior written
permission of the publishers.

First printing August 1988
Second printing October 1988

National Library of Australia
Cataloguing-in-Publication data

Pfitzner, John C. (John Clement), 1942 –
    Australian Parables.

    ISBN 0 85910 465 6

    1. Meditations.   I. Title.

242′.2

Printed and published by
Lutheran Publishing House,
205 Halifax Street, Adelaide, South Australia   88-1385

To
John Hannaford
whose talk at a conference
sparked the idea of searching for
Australian images to present the Gospel;
and to
the members of Immanuel Church, North
Adelaide, the first to hear these 'parables'.

Introduction

The 'parables' in this book are an attempt to present the Christian message in a way that is clear, vivid, and fresh. In writing them I have made use of stories, images, and analogies, similar to Jesus' use of parables in his teaching. Because they are meant for my fellow-Australians, I have particularly explored our own situation, our own 'mythology' here in Australia, for stories and images to carry the message of what God has done for us through Jesus Christ.

The Good News of Jesus continues to speak to people of all times and all places with its exciting message of hope and new life. I hope that these 'parables' will show that God has an exciting message also for us Aussies.

John Pfitzner
Easter, 1988

Acknowledgments

Grateful acknowledgment is hereby expressed for the use of the following copyright material:

Extracts from *Ash Road* by Ivan Southall, © Ivan Southall 1965, used by permission of the author and Angus & Robertson Publishers.

Extracts from *Over the Top* by Ivan Southall, © Ivan Southall 1972, used by permission of the author.

Scripture quotations from the *Good News Bible: Today's English Version* (TEV), © 1976 by the American Bible Society, and from the *New International Version* (NIV), © 1978 by the New York International Bible Society.

Photo Credits appear on the last page of this book.

Approaching Brachina, Flinders Ranges, SA

Contents

Flynn of the Inland and the Flying Doctor............................... 7
Lost in the Bush 12
Food-drop in the Flooded Outback 17
Don Bradman... 20
The Lighthouse at Port Adelaide 23
Once a Jolly Swagman.. 26
Ernest Giles and the Crossing of the Great Victoria Desert.......... 30
The Breaking of the Drought... 35
The Expert on Snakes.. 38
Simpson and His Donkey 42
Saturday Afternoon at the Footy 46
The Bushfire 49
Matthew Flinders and the *Investigator* 53
The Pardoned Convict.. 57
Sunrise in Central Australia 61
Peter Lalor and the Eureka Stockade 65
Ayers Rock 70
The Man from Snowy River... 74
The Outback Missionary 79
World War I Volunteers... 83
The Australian Cuckoo 88
Catherine Helen Spence and Voting Rights for Women.............. 91
Cyclone Tracy.. 95
Gold Rush.. 99
Colonel William Light and the City of Adelaide 102
Winning the Premiership.. 105
Survival in the Outback 109
The Convict and the Parson 113
Killing the Snake 117
The Hurricane Lamp in the Storm 121
Charles Kingsford Smith and the *Southern Cross*.................... 124
The Chinese on the Australian Goldfields 129
The Queenstown Mine Disaster....................................... 133
John McDouall Stuart and the Overland Telegraph Line 137
Drought Conditions in the Mallee.................................... 141
Our Olympic Gold Medallists 145
Captain Cook and Possession Island.................................. 149
Tragedy on Lake Alexandrina... 152
Edward John Eyre and the Aboriginal Guide 156
Photo Credits 160

Flynn of the Inland and the Flying Doctor

There is a painting by the Australian artist Frederick McCubbin entitled *A Bush Burial* (1890). In a small clearing in the bush, only four people and a dog stand around the grave — a man and his wife, their young daughter, and an old man in ordinary clothes reading from a book.

The picture says something about the hardships and dangers of life in the bush in the early days of settlement here in Australia. The fact that there are so few people at the funeral shows that they are in some isolated and remote place, too far away for other people to attend, too remote, perhaps, even to contact other people. One can't help feeling, especially from the woman's reaction, that it's a child being buried. Perhaps the child died because of their isolation — they were too far away from medical help.

One man who tried to do something about the problems and dangers involved in living in the bush was a Presbyterian minister called John Flynn — Flynn of the Inland, to most Australians. Flynn came to see the needs of people living in the outback while serving as a minister in the northern parts of South Australia. People who knew him have spoken of his compassion as one of his most striking characteristics. He was concerned that too many people died lonely and unnecessary deaths in the bush. He was particularly concerned that women and children living in the bush should have security.

Flynn had a dream. It was the dream of providing for the people in the outback what he called a 'mantle of safety'. He wanted to provide a means of communication for them, and access to medical help when it was needed. He devoted his life to achieving this dream. His work led to the establishing of the Royal Flying Doctor Service, which still operates to this day.

Jesus was approaching a town called Nain, when he was suddenly confronted by the sad reality of death. A funeral procession was coming out from the gate of the town. A woman who had already lost her husband was now on her way to bury her only child, a grown-up son.

Jesus was filled with compassion for her. He told her to stop crying. Then he stunned the big crowd of people there by showing that he had power even over death. He said to the dead

Royal Flying Doctor Service aeroplane

man: 'Young man! Get up, I tell you!' (Luke 7:14 TEV). The man sat up, alive and well, and Jesus gave him back to his mother.

What Jesus did here was not done just for this widow and her son. This amazing miracle points ahead to the even greater miracle of Jesus' own death and resurrection. This is where Jesus showed compassion also for you and me. This is where he overcame the power of death for all of us. In sending Jesus to die on the cross, God was doing for us what John Flynn did for the people of the outback — he was providing for us a mantle of safety.

In providing his mantle of safety for people in the bush, Flynn saw that the enemy to be overcome was distance, what Geoffrey Blainey in his book about Australia has called 'the tyranny of distance'. It's distance, with the isolation it creates, that brings problems and dangers for people in the outback.

God, too, in providing his mantle of safety for us, had to overcome the problem of distance. This was the distance caused by sin. It's sin that puts us far away from God, that separates and isolates us from him. And it's sin that also brings death, the ultimate separation from God. To overcome the problem of distance between himself and us, God had to overcome the problem of our sin.

Flynn envisaged two ways of overcoming the problem of distance — the wireless and the aeroplane. Wireless would provide a means of communication over long distance. The aeroplane would enable medical help to be brought to people in isolated locations.

As far as wireless was concerned, the problem at first was that the right equipment didn't yet exist. What was needed was a small, portable, tough machine, easy to operate, and with its own power supply.

The problems were finally solved by a brilliant electrical engineer in Adelaide called Alf Traeger. He perfected the pedal wireless, and it became possible for the first time to provide people in the outback with a simple and reliable wireless transceiver.

In providing a mantle of safety for us, God too has provided a means of communication between himself and us. He has done this in his Word, and especially in Jesus, the Word become flesh. In Jesus, God speaks to us and we can speak back to him. That's why we say 'through Jesus Christ our Lord' when we pray. Jesus is like a transceiver through whom we have heard God speaking to us and through whom we can now reply. He overcomes the distance separating us from God, and brings us into contact with him.

The message transmitted by wireless in the outback can be a real life-saving word. A nursing sister was delivering a baby at an Aboriginal mission station, when serious complications developed. During the whole birth, she was in contact by wireless with the doctor in Alice Springs. She told him what was happening, and he advised and directed her. The baby was born safely.

God's Word, spoken to us in Jesus, is a life-saving word too. We see how powerful this Word is in the case of the widow's son. When Jesus said to him: 'Young man! Get up, I tell you!' those words were strong enough to bring him back to life. It's that same powerful and life-giving Word that God speaks to us whenever Jesus comes to us in the Gospel and in Holy Communion.

The other way envisaged by Flynn of overcoming the problem of distance was by means of the aeroplane. Sometimes a doctor had to be able to get to a sick or injured person, or a person had to be evacuated to a hospital for treatment. The Flying Doctor became a crucial part of Flynn's mantle of safety.

In Jesus, God has provided a Flying Doctor for us too. Jesus has come right to us where we are in order to help us. Not only did he become a person of flesh and blood like us, he even died our death. It's when we see Jesus on the cross that we see how close he has come to us.

And it's on the cross that he did his work for us as our doctor. By his death he cured us of the disease of sin. He rescued us from death. He overcame the distance separating us from God because of our sin. He evacuated us from the place of death, and brought us safely under God's protection and care.

If you look up at a light aircraft flying overhead you will see that its body and its wings make the shape of a cross in the sky. The people who lived under Flynn's mantle of safety provided by the Flying Doctor's aeroplane lived under the sign of the cross.

We, too, live under the sign of the cross. The outstretched wings of the aeroplane can remind us of the outstretched arms of Jesus on the cross. It's because of Jesus and his death on the cross that we can live under God's mantle of safety.

God has been an Alf Traeger for us. In Jesus he has provided us with a transceiver, a means of communication between himself and us. He has also been a John Flynn for us. In Jesus he has provided for us a Flying Doctor who can cure us of sin and save us from death. In Jesus, God has overcome the tyranny of distance and provided a mantle of safety for us.

In the face of death, people in the outback have often simply had to put their faith in the wireless, and their only hope has been the Flying Doctor. In the face of death, we can put our faith in Jesus. In the face of sin and death, he is our only hope.

> Soon afterwards Jesus went to a town called Nain, accompanied by his disciples and a large crowd. Just as he arrived at the gate of the town, a funeral procession was coming out. The dead man was the only son of a woman who was a widow, and a large crowd from the town was with her. When the Lord saw her, his heart was filled with pity for her, and he said to her, 'Don't cry'. Then he walked over and touched the coffin, and the men carrying it stopped. Jesus said, 'Young man! Get up, I tell you!' The dead man sat up and began to talk, and Jesus gave him back to his mother.
>
> They all were filled with fear and praised God. 'A great prophet has appeared among us!' they said; 'God has come to save his people!'
>
> This news about Jesus went out through all the country and the surrounding territory.
>
> (Luke 7:11–17 TEV)

Lost in the Bush

It's not hard to get lost in the Australian bush. Especially in the early days of settlement, it was not uncommon for children to get lost, and this was something parents in remote places were constantly worried about.

There is a story about the search for a lost child in Tom Collins' classic Australian novel *Such Is Life*. The story is told to a group of bushmen yarning around the campfire one evening by Steve Thompson, one of the characters in the novel, who took part in the search.

The five-year-old girl had got lost when she apparently went out to look for her father. He had been away for three days mustering sheep. A dead man had been found in the scrub near their hut not long before, and this had apparently played on the girl's mind and made her anxious about her father. On the morning of the third day, the girl's mother had come back from milking the goats and had found that the girl was gone. She searched for her for an hour. In the hut, she found that a billy of milk and half a loaf of bread were missing.

When she couldn't find the girl, she set out to walk the 12 miles through the bush to the station homestead. There the boss's wife managed to get a horse in from the paddock, and she then rode out to the ewe-paddock to look for the men. It was late in the afternoon when the first men were contacted. They immediately rode off in various directions to pass on the message to as many people as they could.

It was late that evening when a man brought the message to where Steve Thompson and several other men were camped, that Dan O'Connell's little girl was lost in the scrub on Goolumbulla. The men started out immediately, and rode all through the night to the station homestead. The search really began only the next morning after the girl had been out for 24 hours.

One of the men who joined the search was a man they called Barefooted Bob. He was a rough character whom nobody liked, but he was a good bushman. On the way to Dan O'Connell's hut, Bob picked up the girl's tracks, and he was off his horse in an instant following them on foot. They managed to follow the tracks that day for about 12 or 14 miles. A man followed Bob, ringing a cowbell from time to time to signal the line he was following, while other men spread out on horseback in front and to either side.

At nightfall, the search had to come to a halt. Progress next day was frustratingly slow, as they kept losing the track among sheep pads. They were at a complete standstill, when a man drove up in a buggy with an Aboriginal woman. Men had been out all the time looking for Aborigines, but just at that time hadn't been able to find any. Thompson says:

> She was an old, grey-haired lubra, blind of one eye; but she knew her business, and she was on the job for life or death. She picked up the track at a glance, and run it like a bloodhound.

They could tell they were getting close, but weren't able to find the girl before nightfall.

Thompson speaks of what that night was like:

> Longest night I ever passed, though it was one of the shortest in the year. Eyes burning for want of sleep, and couldn't bear to lie down for a minute. Wandering about for miles; listening; hearing something in the scrub, and finding it was only one of the other chaps, or some sheep. Thunder and lightning, on and off, all night; even two or three drops of rain, toward morning. Once I heard the howl of a dingo, and I thought of the little girl, lying worn-out, half-asleep and half-fainting — far more helpless than a sheep — and I made up my mind that if she came out safe I would lead a better life for the future.

The search was resumed at first light next morning. They were getting really close, and actually heard the girl feebly calling for her father. Men were riding everywhere, but couldn't find her in the thick scrub.

Thompson was with Bob and the Aboriginal woman, still following the tracks.

> We were crossing fresh horse-tracks every few yards; and never two minutes but what somebody turned up to ask the news. But to show how little use anything was except fair tracking, the lubra herself never saw the child till she went right up to where she was lying between two thick, soft bushes that met over her, and hid her from sight.

They were half an hour too late. The girl had fallen into a bandicoot burrow and had been too weak to lift her face out of the loose earth.

If Jesus had lived in Australia, he might well have told a story about a child lost in the bush. But this sort of thing probably didn't happen in Galilee, so instead he told a story about a man who had a hundred sheep, and when one of them got lost he went looking for it and was really happy when he finally found it again. And he told another story about a woman who lost a precious coin, and who looked high and low for it, and was so happy when she finally found it that she threw a party.

In telling these stories, Jesus was really talking about *people* who were lost. This is clear from what he says at the end of the story of the lost sheep: 'I tell you, there will be more joy in heaven over one sinner who repents than over ninety-nine respectable people who do not need to repent' (Luke 15:7 TEV). God celebrates when a lost person is found.

Jesus told these stories because the religious leaders of his day were criticizing him for welcoming social and religious outcasts and eating with them. In telling these stories, he was defending his actions against those who found them objectionable. 'God', he said, 'is concerned about those who are lost. He has sent me out to look for them.'

Steve Thompson and the other men had no hesitation in joining the search for the lost girl. They immediately gave up any other plans they had, and were prepared to go without sleep and endure all kinds of hardship in order to find her. We would do the same. In that situation nobody says: 'It's only a child, what's all the fuss about? It was probably her own fault, so why should it concern me?' Such an attitude would be condemned by everyone as cruel and inhuman. It doesn't matter who it is, it's a human life and it's precious, and we do everything we can to find the child and save her life.

But it is possible for us to have an inhuman and uncaring attitude to the people around us who are lost in a different way. These are the people who in one way or another have made a mess of their lives and got into trouble, the ones who don't measure up to our moral or religious standards, the social and religious outcasts of our day. Often our attitude to these people is like that of the religious leaders of Jesus' day. We grizzle about them, we criticize them and say it's their own fault and it serves them right, we wipe them off.

This is a special danger for us respectable people. We start to think of ourselves as better than others, and we look down on those who don't make the grade. We become hard, uncaring, inhuman, like people refusing to join in the search for a lost girl. And if the girl is finally found safe and sound, we don't join in the celebrations because we didn't care if she perished in the bush anyway.

We must never forget that we were lost too. We were like stupid children who disobeyed their father and got themselves hopelessly lost in the bush. But God wasn't harsh or inhuman in his attitude toward us. He didn't say: 'Serves you right'. He worried about us and was concerned for our safety. He sent the best person he could to come looking for us.

The best person for finding children lost in the bush has always been the Aborigine. In Thompson's story, the first question asked when news of the lost child was brought was: 'Anybody know where there's any blackfellows?' Without the Aboriginal woman, the girl would almost certainly never have been found, because just after they found her the storm broke, obliterating all tracks. Speaking of the Aboriginal woman's tracking ability, Thompson says: 'Very rarely — hardly ever — we could see what signs the lubra was following.' And again: 'You see, we were nowhere beside Bob, and Bob was nowhere beside the old lubra'. Many people lost in the bush have owed their lives to the skill of the black-tracker.

When God wanted to find us, he sent the best black-tracker of them all. Jesus was the only one with the skill and the ability to track us down in the scrub and bring us to safety. He was the only one who could bring us back to God.

It wasn't an easy thing for Jesus to do. Like the Aborigine, he was despised and rejected. But he gave it everything he had. He was prepared to endure hardship and suffering for our sake. His search for us led him to the cross, where he ended up giving his life for us.

But he found us all right. He brought us back safe and sound to our Father. And God was happy. He is so thrilled and excited that he celebrates our return.

We need to keep remembering how we were lost and how we were found by Jesus. We need to keep learning that every human life is precious to God, and that he has a special care and concern for those who are lost. We need to keep learning from Jesus how to be a tracker, how to find and help those still lost in the scrub.

Jesus didn't find us so that we could take it easy at the homestead with our feet up, drinking beer. He found us so that we could join in the search for those who are still lost. That's where he is, out there in the scrub, and that's where he wants us to be too.

> One day when many tax collectors and other outcasts came to listen to Jesus, the Pharisees and the teachers of the Law started grumbling, 'This man welcomes outcasts and even eats with them!' So Jesus told them this parable:
>
> 'Suppose one of you has a hundred sheep and loses one of them — what does he do? He leaves the other ninety-nine sheep in the pasture and goes looking for the one that got lost until he finds it. When he finds it, he is so happy that he puts it on his shoulders and carries it back home. Then he calls his friends and neighbours together and says to them, "I am so happy I found my lost sheep. Let us celebrate!" In the same way, I tell you, there will be more joy in heaven over one sinner who repents than over ninety-nine respectable people who do not need to repent.
>
> 'Or suppose a woman who has ten silver coins loses one of them — what does she do? She lights a lamp, sweeps her house, and looks carefully everywhere until she finds it. When she finds it, she calls her friends and neighbours together, and says to them, "I am so happy I found the coin I lost. Let us celebrate!" In the same way, I tell you, the angels of God rejoice over one sinner who repents.'
>
> (Luke 15:1–10 TEV)

Food-drop in the Flooded Outback

An exciting event took place for me when we were living in central Australia. It happened during the big floods of January 1974, when many people in the outback were cut off by floodwaters and had to be supplied from the air.

I was at Palm Valley in the hills south from Hermannsburg. The mechanic at Hermannsburg had built a raft from 44-gallon drums, and he and I had travelled on it down the flooded Finke River to Palm Valley.

Apart from a thirst for adventure, we had wanted to make contact with the Palm Valley ranger, who was living with his wife and their small baby in a caravan near the Amphitheatre. They had been there, cut off by floodwaters, and without radio contact, for two weeks. After we got there, however, more heavy rain fell, the river came up in full flood again, and we were trapped there with them for several days.

One morning, a light aircraft came in low making a preliminary pass overhead to check the location of the caravan and the best place to make a food-drop. Then it disappeared for a time, as it made a wide turn over Palm Paddock.

Suddenly we caught sight of it again, as it came in over the top of Battleship Rock. Then it dropped down low, with the engine throttled right back. As it passed overhead, suddenly a large round bundle fell out of the open door of the plane and plummeted to the ground — the food had been packed in hay inside a large hessian sack. The sack split open as it hit the ground, and its contents were sent flying forward over a wide area of spinifex and bushes. We spent the next half hour excitedly retrieving everything.

I remember feeling very moved at the time by this event. People in Alice Springs, 120 km away, had gone to all this trouble to provide for us in this remote place out in the wilderness. It was like a rescue operation. We were completely cut off, completely isolated. But because of the food-drop we would be all right, we would survive.

Jesus had gone out into the wilderness, to a lonely place, to be by himself. But huge crowds of people had followed him. When he saw them *his heart was filled with pity for them, and he healed those who were ill.*

That evening his disciples came to him and said, 'It is already very late, and this is a lonely place. Send the people away and let them go to the villages to buy food for themselves.'

'They don't have to leave', answered Jesus. 'You yourselves give them something to eat!'

'All we have here are five loaves and two fish', they replied.

'Then bring them here to me', Jesus said. He ordered the people to sit down on the grass; then he took the five loaves and the two fish, looked up to heaven, and gave thanks to God. He broke the loaves and gave them to the disciples, and the disciples gave them to the people.

Everyone ate and had enough. Then the disciples took up twelve baskets full of what was left over. The number of men who ate was about five thousand, not counting the women and children.

(Matthew 14:14–21 TEV)

Out there in the wilderness Jesus carried out a kind of rescue operation. When the people were hungry and had nothing to eat, he came to their rescue by providing food for them.

He has done the same kind of thing for us. When we were cut off and completely isolated from God, when we were without food and in danger of perishing, God mounted a rescue operation for us. He sent Jesus on a long journey to locate us in the wilderness and supply us with food. His coming has saved our life.

There was an earlier time when God fed his people in the desert. It was part of his great act of rescue in liberating his people from forced labour in Egypt. During their 40 years of travelling in the wilderness from Egypt to Canaan, he provided a daily food-drop for them. 'I am going to make food rain down from the sky' (Exod. 16:4 TEV), he had said, and every day the people were able to gather from the ground the flaky, white, sweet stuff called manna.

Now the same kind of thing is happening again. Jesus' feeding of the people in the wilderness is an exciting event because it signals that God is in the process of mounting a new rescue operation. People are again being fed out in the wilderness as part of a great new act of rescue.

Rescue operations can be very costly. It costs a lot of money to put planes in the air and send them long distances with food for people in danger of their lives in remote places.

It cost God a lot to mount his rescue operation for you and me. He spared nothing. He gave everything he had. It was a difficult and dangerous undertaking, which cost him the life of his Son.

It was on the cross that God successfully carried through his great rescue operation for us. This is where Jesus came and found us, when we were completely cut off from God by the floodwaters of our own sin. This is where God made his life-saving food-drop for us, and saved us from perishing.

What Jesus did in feeding the people out in the wilderness is similar to what he did when he ate the Last Supper with his disciples just before he was crucified. On that occasion, too, he took the bread, gave thanks to God, and then gave it to the disciples. In giving the bread he said: 'This is my body, given for you'. In giving the wine he said: 'This is my blood, shed for you for the forgiveness of sins'.

The food that Jesus brings us as part of his rescue operation is really himself, his own body and blood given for us on the cross. He himself is the food-drop from God that saves our life.

Jesus started with only five loaves and two fish, but everyone ended up having more than enough to eat. There were even 12 baskets full of leftovers.

God doesn't skimp when he makes his food-drop for us in Jesus. He provides more than enough for all our needs. There is always lots left over for us to share with one another, and to pass on to others who are still isolated and in trouble.

I'll never forget how excited we were at Palm Valley as we hunted for the tins and packets of food in the spinifex and bushes. It felt like Christmas. And that night in the caravan, out there in the wilderness cut off by the floodwaters, we sat down to a feast.

It's an exciting thing to be a Christian and to keep on discovering the good things God keeps sending us in Christ. Out here in the wilderness, surrounded by dangers, we can keep sitting down with each other to enjoy the great eucharistic feast he has provided for us.

Don Bradman

On August 27, 1908, at Cootamundra in New South Wales, a son was born to Mr and Mrs Bradman. They decided to name him Donald George. They had no idea at that time, of course, that the name of Don Bradman would become the greatest name in cricket.

Today in the world of cricket Don Bradman's name stands above all other names. This is simply because of his outstanding achievements as a cricketer. He rewrote the record books. As a batsman, he was in a class of his own. He was the champion of champions.

This is why his name is always mentioned with respect, admiration, and praise. Johnnie Moyes said of him: 'Bradman was the champion of all time. He set the fields blazing with the burning heat of his genius.' England captain Wally Hammond has said: 'If I were choosing a side out of all the cricketers who have ever lived, I would put Bradman's name down first. None of us had the measure of him and that's the plain fact.'

In his Letter to the Philippians, the apostle Paul speaks of another person whose name stands above all other names. He is speaking of Jesus. 'God exalted him to the highest place and gave him the name that is above every name' (Phil. 2:9 NIV).

When Mary and Joseph had their baby circumcised, according to Jewish custom, a week after his birth, they gave him the name Jesus, the name Mary had been told to give him by the angel. They could hardly have imagined that the name of their child would become the greatest name in all history.

How has it happened that the name of Jesus has become greater than any other name? Don Bradman made a name for himself with his amazing achievements on the cricket field. Time and again, it was his great innings which saved Australia and gave them victory. The statistics show that he was simply the greatest, that he was a true champion.

It's the same with Jesus, whose name is greater than any other name. He made a name for himself by what he did, by what he achieved. His greatest achievement was his death for us on the cross. He did here what no one else has ever done or could have done. Through his death and resurrection he has saved us from defeat at the hands of our opponents — sin and death — and has brought us victory over them. This is what makes him the greatest champion of all time.

That's why we praise him. Bradman's name cannot be mentioned without evoking respect, admiration, and praise. It's the same with Jesus. Wherever he and his great achievements are known, the mention of his name results in honour and praise. St Paul says: 'At the name of Jesus every knee should bow, in heaven and on earth and under the earth, and every tongue confess that Jesus Christ is Lord, to the glory of God the Father' (Phil. 2:10,11). To say that Jesus Christ is Lord is simply to say that he is champion of champions, the greatest of them all.

Bradman's triumphs were shared by a whole nation, by all Australians. On the few occasions he failed, the whole nation was plunged into gloom. When he succeeded, everyone shared the glory and the triumph.

You and I are involved in a similar way in what Jesus did. Defeat for him would have meant defeat for us. His victory, through his death and resurrection, means glory and triumph for us. He did all the hard work, but we enjoy all the benefits.

But there is also something for us to do. St Paul goes on to say 'Continue to work out your salvation with fear and trembling' (Phil. 2:12). The salvation is already ours, but we need to carry it right through to the end.

What St Paul means is that we need to stick with Jesus, through the bad times as well as the good, right to the end, without giving up. We need to keep following him. We need to keep looking to him as our champion.

To keep sharing in Don Bradman's triumphs you simply had to keep on being an Australian barracker. You had to remain a true and loyal supporter, even when things were going badly. In the same way, St Paul encourages us to remain true and loyal followers of Christ, also in the bad times, so that we can continue to share his triumphs right to the end.

In this case, of course, a lot more is at stake than winning a cricket match. Our whole life, our whole future, is at stake, and the opponents we face are very powerful. That's why we have to take this seriously and work at it 'with fear and trembling'. As far as our salvation is concerned, everything depends on Christ. That's why it's crucial that we stick with him and don't ever give up on him.

It is said that Bradman's exploits as a cricketer did a great deal for the nation's morale during the hard days of the Depression and the difficult years during and after the War. The nation had a champion, and this did a lot to lift people's spirits and make life happier. It helped to make their hardships more bearable.

Life can still be hard. We sometimes have to go through sad and difficult times. But in Jesus we have a champion. This is what lifts our spirits. This is what gives us happiness and hope.

Jesus' name gives us something to get excited about, something to share with others who might not be in the know. This name, which is greater than any other name, is our comfort, our joy, and our strength. No matter what happens, we can be confident, because with Jesus we know that we have a true champion on our side, a real winner.

> Therefore God exalted him to the highest place
>   and gave him the name that is above every name,
> that at the name of Jesus every knee should bow,
>   in heaven and on earth and under the earth,
> and every tongue confess that Jesus Christ is Lord,
>   to the glory of God the Father.
>   Therefore, my dear friends, as you have always obeyed — not only in my presence, but now much more in my absence — continue to work out your salvation with fear and trembling, for it is God who works in you to will and to act according to his good purpose.
>
> (Philippians 2:9–13 NIV)

The Lighthouse at Port Adelaide

People were wearing badges which said: 'I saw the light at Port Adelaide'. It didn't mean that they'd had some kind of conversion experience. It was publicity for the new South Australian Maritime Museum at Port Adelaide, which includes, as one of its outdoor exhibits, the big metal lighthouse prominently situated at the end of Commercial Road near No. 1 Wharf.

The lighthouse was built in 1869, and was first used to mark the entrance to Port Adelaide. Then for a long period until 1985, when it was brought back to be part of the museum, it was positioned on Neptune Island outside the entrance to Spencer Gulf.

This lighthouse, like many others around our coastline, was built in order to save lives. By beaming its light out into the darkness, it enabled ships to find their way through treacherous waters and avoid shipwreck.

The prophet Isaiah in the Old Testament speaks of a great light suddenly shining in the darkness: 'The people who walked in darkness have seen a great light. They lived in a land of shadows, but now light is shining on them' (Isa. 9:2 TEV).

He sees this great light coming with the birth of a child, a child who will be a great king like his ancestor King David: 'A child is born to us! A son is given to us! And he will be our ruler.' The greatness of this royal child is shown by the titles he will receive: '"Wonderful Counsellor", "Mighty God", "Eternal Father", "Prince of Peace"' (v 6).

The birth of this child will bring great happiness to the people: 'You have given them great joy, Lord; you have made them happy. They rejoice in what you have done, as people rejoice when they harvest their corn or when they divide captured wealth' (v 3).

They are so happy because, in sending this newborn king, God is rescuing them from the enemy that threatened them: 'You have defeated the nation that oppressed and exploited your people'. 'The boots of the invading army and all their bloodstained clothing will be destroyed by fire' (vv 4,5).

At a dark time in the life of his people, when they lived in the shadow of foreign domination at the hands of Assyria, God sent a powerful light to shine for them in the darkness. The newborn King would be a lighthouse for them, a beacon of safety in the darkness to save them from disaster.

Isaiah's words have come true for us in Jesus, in the birth of the baby born to Mary in Bethlehem. With the birth of Jesus, God has caused a great light to suddenly shine in our darkness. This royal child is the lighthouse that shines in the darkness for us and saves us from disaster.

A lighthouse is of no use to anyone in the middle of a well-lit city, or in some safe, sheltered place far inland. To do its job, it has to be out where it's dark and dangerous — on a lonely headland, or on the bare, exposed rock of Neptune Island, taking the full brunt of the storms off the Southern Ocean.

In being born as a baby at Bethlehem, in coming to be a lighthouse for us, God takes his place here with us where it is darkest and most dangerous. He takes his place in the darkness of cot-deaths and cancer; in the darkness of drug-abuse and the road-toll; in the darkness of prejudice and intolerance; in the darkness of senseless acts of violence and destruction; in the darkness of poverty and oppression; in the darkness of damage to the environment, and the threat of a nuclear winter.

It was on the cross that Jesus stood out in the pitch darkness, taking the full brunt of the storm for us. But it was here that he did his job as our lighthouse. It's from the cross that the powerful light of his love shines out most brightly, piercing through the darkness of sin and evil and death.

The cross of Christ is the storm-battered lighthouse that penetrates the darkness for us and saves us from disaster. With this life-saving light to guide us, we can ride the storm and find a safe passage.

In the darkness and in the storm, look for the lighthouse that God has given us in the child born at Bethlehem. Look for the light that shines from the cross of Christ. This is the only light that can overcome the darkness in our life.

Direct your fellow-sailors to this lighthouse, so that they can share with us the relief and joy of finding this light. It's the only light that can save us and our world from shipwreck.

> *The people who walked in darkness*
> *have seen a great light.*
> *They lived in a land of shadows,*
> *but now light is shining on them.*

Lighthouse at Port Adelaide, SA

You have given them great joy, Lord;
  you have made them happy.
They rejoice in what you have done,
  as people rejoice when they harvest their corn
  or when they divide captured wealth.
For you have broken the yoke that burdened them
  and the rod that beat their shoulders.
You have defeated the nation
  that oppressed and exploited your people,
  just as you defeated the army of Midian long ago.
The boots of the invading army
  and all their bloodstained clothing
  will be destroyed by fire.
A child is born to us!
  A son is given to us!
  And he will be our ruler.
He will be called 'Wonderful Counsellor',
  'Mighty God', 'Eternal Father',
  'Prince of Peace'.
His royal power will continue to grow;
  his kingdom will always be at peace.
He will rule as King David's successor,
  basing his power on right and justice,
  from now until the end of time.
The Lord Almighty is determined to do all this.

(Isaiah 9:2–7 TEV)

Once a Jolly Swagman

There was once a rich squatter who owned a big area of some of the finest grazing land in New South Wales, on which he ran several thousand head of sheep. With the money he made from wool he was able to build a magnificent homestead, where he and his family lived very comfortably.

There was a swagman called Larry, who used to call at the homestead from time to time for a handout. He usually arranged to call at about sundown, so that he could get a feed without having to do any work. He was a lazy, good-for-nothing sort of bloke, with a reputation for being a petty thief. Sometimes when he called at the homestead he would get something to eat, but other times, if the boss caught sight of him, he'd have the dogs sooled on to him and he'd have to run for it.

The swagman died in rather unusual circumstances. The squatter suspected him of having pinched a sheep, so he called in the troopers. They caught him redhanded down at the creek where he was camped, boiling his billy under a coolibah tree. He tried to escape by jumping in the billabong, but unfortunately he got drowned.

Nobody knew where he came from or whether he had any next-of-kin, so he was buried without ceremony in a corner of the town graveyard, with only the local JP and the grave-digger present.

The squatter lived to a ripe old age. He became one of the wealthiest, most influential and admired men in the district. When he finally died, his funeral was the biggest anyone could remember in those parts. Speeches were made about what a fine man he'd been, and the tremendous contributions he'd made to the progress and prosperity of the region.

But after their death their situations changed. Larry, the disreputable swaggie, was admitted to paradise, where he had a great time boiling the billy and swapping yarns with Abraham and the other patriarchs. But the rich squatter, admired and respected by everybody, ended up in hell.

That's my Australian version of a story Jesus once told. Jesus' story is about 'a rich man who dressed in the most expensive clothes and lived in great luxury every day' (Luke 16:19 TEV). There's also 'a poor man named Lazarus, covered with sores, who

Aboriginal waterhole, Kanyaka, SA

used to be brought to the rich man's door, hoping to eat the bits of food that fell from the rich man's table' (v 20). When the poor man died, he 'was carried by the angels to sit beside Abraham at the feast in heaven' (v 22). But when the rich man died, he ended up in great pain in the fires of hell.

Why did it happen like that? Why was the successful man of good standing in the community punished, and the no-hoper rewarded?

Jesus wants to tell us that in our relationship with God there's a sense in which it's better to be a beggar than a rich man, better to be a swagman than a squatter.

The trouble with being a squatter is that my wealth, my social standing, my comfortable life can make it hard for me to relate to God in a right way. They can lull me into a false sense of security. They can make me feel that my worth is determined by my wealth, and that God, like everyone else, will be impressed by what I've made of my life. My money and possessions can make me feel that I've got everything I need, that I've got nothing to worry about, that I'm safe, that I don't really need God. There's also the danger that I become hard and uncaring toward people like Larry.

The truth of the matter is that in relation to God we are not respectable squatters. Instead, we are disreputable swagmen. Jesus' story makes it clear that the rich man's wealth and social standing counted for nothing in God's eyes. God looks deeper than that. As far as God is concerned, we are all beggars. We are people with nothing — nothing to pay him with, nothing to brag about, nothing that will impress him or put him in our debt. We are sinners, not good and respectable people, but rogues, crooks, scoundrels, no-hopers, people who are good-for-nothing.

If that's what I am really like, how can I survive? How can I avoid ending up in hell?

The only way swagmen survived in the early days was on the handouts they received. It's the same for us. The only way we can survive is on the handouts we receive from God. That's the only way we can escape death and hell. Our only hope is in God's goodness and grace.

When we think of handouts, we usually think of something pretty meagre — left-overs, a few sandwiches, just the bare necessities, a subsistence diet, nothing too exciting. But it's not like that with the handouts we get from God. When God gives a handout he really knows how to lay it on — a whole sugarbag full of the best things from the pantry.

At the end of Jesus' story, the rich man asks Abraham to send Lazarus to his five brothers to warn them. He's worried that they'll end up in hell too. But Abraham says to him: 'Your brothers have Moses and the prophets to warn them; your brothers should listen to what they say' (Luke 16:29). He's saying that in God's Word they have everything they need to escape hell, if only they will realize it.

It's in his Word that God makes his handouts to us. What he gives us here is such good food because it contains the Gospel, the Good News. Through this Word he gives us Jesus, who conquered sin, death, and hell for us through his death and resurrection. This is real life-saving food. It gives us eternal life in fellowship with God. With this food, we can survive in the face of death and hell.

That's why it's not a bad thing to be a beggar, a swagman, before God. Because when we come to him with nothing, with empty hands, then we can receive the really good handouts he gives us in Christ. Being a swaggie means living my life relying completely on God's goodness and grace. It means that God's Word, the Gospel, becomes my staple diet.

And once I've discovered for myself where the best handouts are to be found, then I've got some really good news to pass on to the other poor beggars out on the track still looking for a feed.

'There was once a rich man who dressed in the most expensive clothes and lived in great luxury every day. There was also a poor man named Lazarus, covered with sores, who used to be brought to the rich man's door, hoping to eat the bits of food that fell from the rich man's table. Even the dogs would come and lick his sores.

The poor man died and was carried by the angels to sit beside Abraham at the feast in heaven. The rich man died and was buried, and in Hades, where he was in great pain, he looked up and saw Abraham, far away, with Lazarus at his side. So he called out, "Father Abraham! Take pity on me, and send Lazarus to dip his finger in some water and cool my tongue, because I am in great pain in this fire!"

But Abraham said, "Remember, my son, that in your lifetime you were given all the good things, while Lazarus got all the bad things. But now he is enjoying himself here, while you are in pain. Besides all that, there is a deep pit lying between us, so that those who want to cross over from here to you cannot do so, nor can anyone cross over to us from where you are." The rich man said, "Then I beg you, father Abraham, send Lazarus to my father's house, where I have five brothers. Let him go and warn them so that they, at least, will not come to this place of pain."

Abraham said, "Your brothers have Moses and the prophets to warn them; your brothers should listen to what they say." The rich man answered, "That is not enough, father Abraham! But if someone were to rise from death and go to them, then they would turn from their sins." But Abraham said, "If they will not listen to Moses and the prophets, they will not be convinced even if someone were to rise from death".'

(Luke 16:19–31 TEV)

Ernest Giles and the Crossing of the Great Victoria Desert

Ernest Giles called himself the last of the explorers, and it's true that as a result of his five expeditions the last big gaps in the map of Australia were finally filled in.

Probably his most remarkable achievement was his crossing in 1875 of the Great Victoria Desert, the area north of the Nullarbor Plain. He was using camels for the first time, and with his party of seven men he had reached a small waterhole just the other side of the Western Australian border. They called the waterhole Boundary Dam.

Here Giles was faced with a critical decision. He had reconnoitred further west, and had found no sign of water. The Boundary Dam waterhole was quickly drying up. He had to decide whether he would go on into the desert, or whether he would retreat back into South Australia.

The decision he made can be seen as either very courageous or very foolhardy. He decided to go ahead and attempt a crossing of the desert, trusting in the camels, and hoping to find water somewhere on the way. He decided to head straight for Mount Churchman, a hill north-east of Perth, 650 miles away, where he knew there was water.

He told the other members of his party what he intended doing, and gave them the choice of following him or of going back. They were warned that if they followed him they could very well be going to their death. He described the event in his journal in this way:

> I informed my officers and men that I had determined to push westward, without a thought of retreat, no matter what the result might be; that it was a matter of life or death for us; we must push through or die in the scrubs. I added that if any more than one of the party desired to retreat, I would provide them with rations and camels, when they could either return to Fowler's Bay by the way we had come, or descend to Eucla Station on the coast, which lay south nearly 170 miles distant.
>
> I represented that we were probably in the worst desert upon the face of the earth, but that fact should give us all the more pleasure in conquering it. We were surrounded on all

sides by dense scrubs, and the sooner we forced our way out of them the better. It was of course a desperate thing to do, and I believe very few people would or could rush madly into a totally unknown wilderness, where the nearest known water was 650 miles away. But I had sworn to go to Perth or die in the attempt, and I inspired the whole of my party with my own enthusiasm. One and all declared that they would live or die with me.

There came a time for Jesus' disciples when they were faced with a crucial decision similar to the one made by Giles's men at Boundary Dam.

Jesus had asked them: 'Who do the crowds say I am?' They had answered: 'Some say that you are John the Baptist. Others say that you are Elijah, while others say that one of the prophets of long ago has come back to life.' 'What about you?' Jesus asked them. 'Who do you say I am?' Peter, speaking for all of them, answered: 'You are God's Messiah' (Luke 9:18–20) TEV).

A critical point had been reached. They had come to know the secret of who Jesus really was — that he was the Messiah, the promised rescuer sent by God. Where would they go from here?

It's at this critical moment that Jesus decides that he must inform them of what lies ahead — for himself as the Messiah, and for them as his followers. It's only fair that they should know. He tells them: 'The Son of Man must suffer much and be rejected by the elders, the chief priests, and the teachers of the Law. He will be put to death, but three days later he will be raised to life' (Luke 9:22). The way ahead for Jesus himself is the way of suffering and death.

And the situation for his followers is no different. 'If anyone wants to come with me, he must forget self, take up his cross every day, and follow me. For whoever wants to save his own life will lose it, but whoever loses his life for my sake will save it' (vv 23,24).

There were probably men who joined exploration parties expecting to share in the romance, adventure, and glory of going into unexplored country and making new discoveries. But suddenly, as happened at Boundary Dam, they could find themselves faced with the distinct possibility of death in the desert.

The disciples probably imagined that as followers of the Messiah they would share his glory and have all kinds of wonderful experiences. But now they hear that the way ahead involves a cross — hardship, suffering, pain, persecution — and that they must be prepared to lose their life for the sake of Jesus.

To follow Jesus is not always easy. It can be difficult and dangerous. It may mean having to be ready to risk our life.

Why would anyone be willing to follow Jesus if it means suffering and death? We can ask the same thing about Giles and his party. What made them willing to risk death in the desert?

Giles spoke to his men about conquering the desert. He saw himself as being involved in a kind of contest with the country. Either the country would kill them or they would conquer the country. The only way to conquer the country was to go out there and cross it, and this meant being prepared for suffering and even death.

Giles's men were prepared to follow him because they had confidence in him. They trusted him. They believed that he was the man who could conquer the desert and bring them safely through.

He didn't let them down. Although he had warned them that they might all die in the desert, not one man perished on that terrible journey.

Jesus was involved in a contest too. His aim was to conquer the devil, to make inroads into his territory and drive him out. He knew that the only way of conquering the devil's territory was to go out there and cross it. But in doing this he had to be prepared to face suffering and death.

We are prepared to follow Jesus because we have confidence in him. We have come to trust him. We believe that he is the one who can overcome the devil and bring us safely through.

The way in which Giles conquered the Great Victoria Desert was quite different from the usual method of exploration. The usual way was to find water, then explore ahead until the next water was found, shift to that place, and then repeat the process. On this occasion, however, Giles did something quite different. He took a compass bearing on Mount Churchman, 650 miles away, and decided simply to keep moving in as straight a line as possible, toward that objective.

It seemed sheer madness, but we know now that it was the only strategy that could have succeeded. There was virtually no water to be found in that whole desert except the one large waterhole they happened to find halfway along their journey. It was only by following that straight line that Giles was able to achieve his objective.

Jesus did something similar in overcoming the devil and conquering his territory. He told his disciples: 'The Son of Man *must* suffer. He *will* be put to death.' He knew that he had to aim straight for the cross if he was going to achieve his objective.

At the very beginning of his ministry, Jesus went out into the desert and there he was tempted by the devil. The devil did everything he could to sidetrack Jesus, to lead him off in all sorts of other directions. But it's as if Jesus, already at that point, had taken a compass bearing on the cross and had made up his mind to follow only that line. Nothing would make him deviate from that course. It was only by following that line that he was able to achieve his objective of overcoming the devil.

When Giles and his men finally reached Perth they were given a hero's welcome. The celebrations went on for two months. Their crossing of the desert was hailed as a triumph, a great victory. The people of Western Australia identified with the achievement and regarded it as a victory for them as well.

Jesus has also achieved a great triumph, a great victory. Through his death and resurrection he has defeated the devil, he has conquered sin and death. This is a victory for everyone, a victory in which all of us can share. It's this great victory that we Christians keep on celebrating.

The way on which Jesus continues to lead us is the way of forgetting self in order to be useful to others. He keeps leading us out into the desert, where things are tough and where there are people who need help. There's nothing very glamorous about it; it's hard work. It can involve pain, and hardship, and opposition.

Don't be frightened to stick with Jesus and to follow where he leads. You can have confidence in him. You can trust him. He promises that not one of those who follow him will be lost. He will take you safely through, and you will share his victory.

One day when Jesus was praying alone, the disciples came to him. 'Who do the crowds say I am?' he asked them.

'Some say that you are John the Baptist', they answered. 'Others say that you are Elijah, while others say that one of the prophets of long ago has come back to life.'

'What about you?' he asked them. 'Who do you say I am?' Peter answered, 'You are God's Messiah'.

Then Jesus gave them strict orders not to tell this to anyone. He also said to them. 'The Son of Man must suffer *much and be rejected by the elders, the chief priests, and the teachers of the Law. He will be put to death, but three days later he will be raised to life.'*

And he said to them all, 'If anyone wants to come with me, he must forget self, take up his cross every day, and follow me. For whoever wants to save his own life will lose it, but whoever loses his life for my sake will save it.'

(Luke 9:18–24 TEV)

The Breaking of the Drought

In a story called 'Drought-Stricken', Henry Lawson writes about conditions in the bush in a time of drought.

> It is a blazing desolation. No sign of crops, no sign of grass, the sods bake white and crumble to dust on the ploughed ground — the surface under the scrub is as bare as a road, and as dusty.

He tells of one man, a selector,

> who, one blazing day, when he thought he was alone, fell on his knees behind a stump, out of sight of the house, and prayed for rain as perhaps man never prayed before. But they have little time for praying out there. They must work on holidays and Sundays in the drought, carting water, lifting weak cattle, and dragging them out of mudholes, cutting down creek-oak and native apple-tree for them to eat, burning the carcasses, and fighting bush fires. It is back-breaking, heart-breaking work.

This is the time when the blue sky seems cruel and pitiless, and the heavens seem to be shut. People wait for the day when the skies will open and the rains will come to break the drought. Lawson writes:

> Haggard eyes stare vainly at every sign of a cloud for rain. The great white sun rises with almost the heat of noon; and so, day after day, week after week, month after month, until people cease to hope, or even to waste words suggesting that it might rain soon. 'Whenever are we going to get a little rain?' says the baked, gaunt bushwoman, wearily — and that is all.

The people living at the time when Jesus was born felt like people who were drought-stricken. In earlier times, God's Spirit had come down on the prophets and they had heard God's voice speaking to them from heaven. But for hundreds of years this hadn't happened any more. God seemed remote. The land seemed barren and dry. The people languished and died.

The skies seemed to be closed. Like people in a drought, they looked to the sky and wondered when the heavens would open, the rain would come, and the drought would break.

It was at this time that Jesus came from Nazareth in the province of Galilee and was baptized by John in the river Jordan. An exciting thing happened. 'As Jesus was coming up out of the water, he saw heaven being torn open ... ' (Mark 1:10 NIV).

At Jesus' baptism the heavens opened. God's Spirit, not seen for so long, came down on Jesus like a dove. And the voice of God, not heard for so many years, was heard from heaven: 'You are my Son, whom I love; with you I am well pleased' (v 11).

What this means for us is that the drought has finally broken. The time of hardship and heartbreak is over. The heavens have finally opened, and the rain has come. God has sent his Son, whom he loves, as the life-giving rain on the parched and barren earth. The land is no longer a place of desolation and death for us, but of new life and new hope.

The terrible hardships experienced by people in drought conditions in early times were sometimes the result of human error, as well as weather conditions. Attempts were made to farm land that was too marginal (in South Australia this was country north of Goyder's Line), the country was overstocked, and the wrong dry-land farming methods were employed.

The spiritual drought from which we suffer is not due to an act of God, but to our own errors and mistakes. We are people who went too far — we crossed God's Goyder's Line where we were not supposed to go, and we've been paying the consequences ever since. It's our own disobedience which closed the heavens and cut us off from God.

The coming of Jesus means the breaking of the drought, because he comes to deal with the problem of our sin. He did this for us on the cross. His baptism in the river Jordan points ahead to this baptism in blood. It was through his death on the cross that he broke the power of sin. Here the heavens were opened for us, and God's grace and love and forgiveness came raining down on us, bringing new life.

At Jesus' baptism, at the very beginning of his ministry, we can already see the final result of his life and work for us. Here in his baptism, where he is called and installed into the special work for which he has been sent, we see that the result of his work, the result of his death and resurrection, will be the opening of the heavens, the sending of God's Spirit, and the hearing of God's voice again.

This has come true for each of us in our own baptism. In the water of our baptism, the drought has broken for us. Here we were united with our crucified and risen Lord, and our sins were forgiven. Here the heavens were opened for us, and God's Spirit came down on us. Here God spoke to me, saying that because of Jesus he was pleased with me and was happy to receive me into his family as his child.

What a transformation of our life this is! Where before there was death and desolation, there is now new growth and new life. The dry and cracked earth of our life is now able to become useful and productive again. As we live our life in fellowship with Christ and in the power of the Holy Spirit, we are constantly refreshed and renewed ourselves, and we are also able to become God's means of bringing refreshment and encouragement to one another.

When your life seems drought-stricken, dry and barren, remember the water of your baptism. Remember how the heavens opened, and the Spirit of God with all his blessings poured down on you. Let the steady rain of Jesus and his forgiveness soak down deep into your cracked and parched soil to bring you new hope, new growth, new vigour, new life.

> *At that time Jesus came from Nazareth in Galilee and was baptized by John in the Jordan. As Jesus was coming up out of the water, he saw heaven being torn open and the Spirit descending on him like a dove. And a voice came from heaven: 'You are my Son, whom I love; with you I am well pleased'.*
>
> (Mark 1:9–11 NIV)

The Expert on Snakes

I was once taken by a friend to a meeting of the Field Naturalists Club in Alice Springs, a small group of people interested in nature and wildlife. One of the talks at this meeting was about snakes, given by a young bloke called Mike Gillam.

Mike was technically not the most accomplished of public speakers, but the talk he gave on that occasion was one of the most interesting I have ever listened to. It was immediately apparent that here was someone who knew what he was talking about. I remember that one of his very first statements was 'None of you people here will ever get bitten by a snake'.

Mike had been interested in reptiles virtually all his life, and there didn't seem to be anything about them that he didn't know. He had a job at that time with the Conservation Commission studying reptiles, particularly snakes — looking for them, catching them, observing them, handling them, learning about them. He was such an expert on snakes because he'd been dealing with them for so long.

When Mike spoke about snakes, everyone sat up and listened, because you could tell straight away that he was an authority on the subject.

The same thing happened when Jesus preached one day in the synagogue in the town of Capernaum. Everyone sat up and listened, because they immediately recognized that here was someone who knew what he was talking about, someone who was an authority. 'The people were amazed at his teaching, because he taught them as one who had authority, not as the teachers of the Law' (Mark 1:22 NIV).

We're not told what Jesus actually spoke about in his sermon, but we are told what happened next. A man with an evil or unclean spirit in him came into the synagogue and screamed: 'What do you want with us, Jesus of Nazareth? Have you come to destroy us? I know who you are — the Holy One of God!' (v 24).

We can imagine the reaction of the people to the sudden appearance of this evil spirit — it would have been like throwing a poisonous snake among them. There would have been pandemonium as people rushed to get out of the way.

Jesus was the one person who didn't flinch. Just as Mike Gillam wasn't scared of snakes because he knew how to handle them, so Jesus wasn't scared of this evil spirit. He knew how to handle it.

He gave a command to the spirit: 'Be quiet! Come out of him!' (v 25). The evil spirit shook the man hard, gave a loud scream, and came out of him.

The people were absolutely stunned. They were amazed at the ease with which Jesus had dealt with the evil spirit. They said to each other: 'What is this? A new teaching — and with authority! He even gives orders to evil spirits and they obey him' (vv 27,28).

The people in the synagogue that day saw that here was someone who spoke and acted with authority. If we were to ask: 'What is Jesus' particular area of expertise, what is he an authority on?', we could answer by saying that just as Mike Gillam was an authority on snakes and how to handle them, so Jesus is an authority on evil spirits and how to deal with them.

Part of the reason we were so interested in Mike's talk on snakes was that snakes are dangerous and we are scared of them. He was able to describe graphically from personal experience the effects of being bitten by a poisonous snake, and what to do to survive snakebite.

The purpose of Jesus' coming was to deal with the things that are dangerous to us and that we are frightened of — all the things the devil can do to hurt us and to destroy us. Jesus came to show us how to survive the devil's snakebite.

How did Jesus come to be such an authority on evil spirits and how to deal with them?

Mike Gillam came to be an expert on snakes by experience. His wasn't merely a theoretical expertise gained from books, but a practical expertise from long experience in actually handling snakes.

Jesus' expertise was of a similar kind. He knew how to handle the devil from personal experience. At the very beginning of his ministry, immediately after he had been baptized by John, he spent a long period in the desert being tempted by the devil. He was able to stand up to that evil spirit in the synagogue because he had already learnt, from personal experience in the desert, how to deal with the devil.

That period of time spent in the desert grappling with the devil, and the incident in the synagogue in Capernaum, show clearly that the whole purpose of Jesus' life and work was to deal with the devil for us, to destroy his power to hurt us.

The evil spirit in the synagogue knew this. That's why he was scared of Jesus. That's why he screamed out: 'What do you want with us, Jesus of Nazareth? Have you come to destroy us?' He knew that with the coming of Jesus, he and his fellow demons were doomed.

Anyone who handles snakes risks getting bitten. Mike had begun his talk by saying that none of us would ever be bitten by a snake. But he went on to say that the people who do get bitten are those who do something stupid, who tackle a snake without knowing what they're doing, or people like himself who regularly handle them.

The friend who took me to the meeting told me that Mike had been bitten so many times that he almost regarded himself as having become immune, and on one occasion when he was bitten again, he didn't bother about getting treatment. It nearly cost him his life. An hour or two later he suddenly started becoming paralyzed and couldn't breathe, and had to be rushed to hospital.

By dealing with evil spirits, by taking on the devil, Jesus also risked getting hurt, he risked getting bitten. This is in fact what happened. It was on the cross that the snake finally got him. That's where the devil inflicted on him all his venom.

But it was there on the cross that Jesus actually showed his real expertise in dealing with snakes. That's where he revealed his full authority over the devil. It was precisely by dying on the cross for us that he milked the devil of his poison. This is where he destroyed the devil's power and rendered him harmless for us.

The water of our baptism, where we were united with our crucified and risen Lord, is our innoculation against snakebite. The body and blood of our Lord, given and shed for us on the cross and received by us in Holy Communion, is the powerful antivenene which makes us immune to the devil's venom. Christ and his cross are our defence against all the evil spirits and whatever they can do to hurt us.

You and I can't deal with the devil. He's far too strong and clever for us, far too dangerous for us to handle. We've got no hope against him.

But in Jesus, God has sent us a Mike Gillam, someone who's an expert on snakes, someone who's an authority on evil spirits and how to handle them, someone who knows how to deal with the devil.

When your life is in danger from the devil, trust the expert, trust Jesus. On the cross he has dealt the devil a crippling blow for us, and because of him we can defy the evil spirits.

> Though devils all the world should fill,
>   All eager to devour us,
> We tremble not, we fear no ill,
>   They shall not overpower us.
>   This world's prince may still
>   Scowl fierce as he will,
>   He can harm us none;
>   He's judged, for e'er undone;
> One little word can fell him.

They went to Capernaum, and when the Sabbath came, Jesus went into the synagogue and began to teach. The people were amazed at his teaching, because he taught them as one who had authority, not as the teachers of the law.

Just then a man in their synagogue who was possessed by an evil spirit cried out, 'What do you want with us, Jesus of Nazareth? Have you come to destroy us? I know who you are — the Holy One of God!'

'Be quiet!' said Jesus sternly. 'Come out of him!'

The evil spirit shook the man violently and came out of him with a shriek.

The people were all so amazed that they asked each other, 'What is this? A new teaching — and with authority! He even gives orders to evil spirits and they obey him.'

News about him spread quickly over the whole region of Galilee.

(Mark 1:21–28 NIV)

Simpson and His Donkey

John Simpson is well known in Australia as the man with the donkey, who carried wounded soldiers out of the battle zone at Gallipoli.

His name was actually John Simpson Kirkpatrick, but when he enlisted in Western Australia with the Third Field Ambulance Medical Corps, he did so simply as John Simpson.

After the landing at Anzac Cove on Gallipoli, he found a donkey at an abandoned Turkish hut, and during the weeks that followed, he used the donkey to bring wounded men down to the beaches from the trenches up on the hills — 12–15 men a day. In the trenches he would give the wounded soldier first-aid, then put him on his donkey and bring him to the field hospital on the beach.

His route up into the hills was along a gully the Australians called 'Shrapnel Gully'. Because it was the main route up into the hills, it was constantly shelled by the Turks and also came under sniper fire. It was here that Simpson was killed on May 19, 1915. He was bringing a wounded man down to the beach, when he was hit by a sniper's bullet. He was 23 years old.

Jesus once told a story about a man with a donkey. A teacher of the Jewish Law had tried to trap him by asking: 'What must I do to receive eternal life?' (Luke 10:25 TEV). Jesus threw the question back at him by saying: 'What do the Scriptures say? How do you interpret them?' (v 26). The man said: ' "Love the Lord your God with all your heart, with all your soul, with all your strength, and with all your mind"; and "Love your neighbour as you love yourself". ' 'You are right', Jesus replied; 'do this and you will live' (vv 27,28).

'But the teacher of the Law wanted to justify himself, so he asked Jesus, "Who is my neighbour?" ' (v 29). In reply Jesus told the parable of the Good Samaritan, about a man with a donkey who stopped to help a Jew who had been bashed up by robbers on the dangerous Jerusalem to Jericho road. He gave him first-aid, then put him on his donkey and took him to an inn, where he paid to have him looked after.

In John Simpson we Australians have our own Good Samaritan. And from men like Simpson we've learnt who our neighbour is. Your neighbour is your mate. We've learnt this in the wars in

'Simpson and his donkey',
sculpture by Peter Corlett
— Australian War Memorial,
Canberra

which we've fought. We also learnt this in the early days of settlement, when people battled to establish themselves in a new and hard land. People in the bush learnt that they had to stick together, they had to help each other.

This is where we learnt the rule, the unwritten law, that you always stick by your mates, that you never let your mates down, that you can depend on them and they can depend on you. And from men like Simpson we learnt that, if necessary, you die for your mates.

We Australians know what it means to be a Good Samaritan. We know who our neighbour is.

But this other man with the donkey, the man in Jesus' story, the Samaritan — the trouble with him is that he *doesn't* know who his neighbour is, he doesn't know who his mates are. Or if he knows, he doesn't seem to care.

He comes along the road and sees a Jew lying there — Jewish scum. The proper thing to do would be to spit on him as he goes past, perhaps even sink the boot in. At the very least he should quickly walk past on the other side of the road.

But that's not what he does. He stops to help him, the stupid idiot. He bandages his wounds, puts him on his donkey, pays good money for him to be looked after. He'll get no thanks for it. This Jew will never admit to his mates that his life was saved by a Samaritan. Samaritan trash would never do a thing like that. He'll tell them it was a priest, or perhaps a Levite, who stopped to help him and who saved his life.

The trouble with this Samaritan is that he goes too far. What if everyone started befriending enemies? It would make a mockery of everything we've ever said about them, the way we've always treated them.

After all, it's stupid to break the rules. It's not only stupid, it's also dangerous. It's a sure way of getting your real mates off-side, of turning your own friends against you.

Just how dangerous it can be is shown by another man with a donkey. There was an occasion when Jesus himself rode into Jerusalem on a donkey. The trouble with Jesus was that he didn't know who his neighbour was either, he didn't know who his mates were. People called him 'sinner lover' because that's the sort of person he made friends with. He made friends with collaborators, prostitutes, social outcasts. And his own people, the people who were his real mates, didn't like it. They were so upset and threatened by it, that they ended up nailing him to a cross.

It doesn't pay to break the rules. It's dangerous. It can be as dangerous as going up Shrapnel Gully.

But — what if I'm the victim? What if I'm the man who's been bashed up and is bleeding to death on the Jericho road? What if I'm the man lying out in no-man's-land with a bullet through me, unable to move? What if I'm one of life's casualties, the one who's lost and hurting?

God didn't walk past you and me when we lay dying. He sent Jesus. He found us, he came to us right where we were. He fixed up our wounds, and carried us to safety. By his death on the cross, he saved our life.

And he did it not for people who were his mates. He did it for people who were his enemies, people who'd turned their backs on him. We were people who had walked past him and gone our own way.

Jesus broke the law for us. He broke the rule which says that you stick by your mates, you help only your mates. He went way beyond what the law required. He broke down the barriers. He treated us, his enemies, as if we were his best mates. He didn't let us down. He gave his own life to save us.

What Jesus has done for us has power to change us. It sets us free to become new people. It has the power to break down the barriers of fear and prejudice we erect around ourselves. It opens our eyes to see each other in new ways, to see past the labels we put on people. It opens our hearts to feel compassion for one another, for those who are hurting, those who are wounded, those who need our help. It gives us the joy of discovering neighbours, friends, mates, where we never knew they existed before.

> A teacher of the Law came up and tried to trap Jesus. 'Teacher', he asked, 'what must I do to receive eternal life?'
>
> Jesus answered him, 'What do the Scriptures say? How do you interpret them?'
>
> The man answered, ' "Love the Lord your God with all your heart, with all your soul, with all your strength, and with all your mind"; and "Love your neighbour as you love yourself".'
>
> 'You are right', Jesus replied; 'do this and you will live.'
>
> But the teacher of the Law wanted to justify himself, so he asked Jesus, 'Who is my neighbour?'
>
> Jesus answered, 'There was once a man who was going down from Jerusalem to Jericho when robbers attacked him, stripped him, and beat him up, leaving him half dead. It so happened that a priest was going down that road; but when he saw the man, he walked on by, on the other side. In the same way a Levite also came along, went over and looked at the man, and then walked on by, on the other side. But a Samaritan who was travelling that way came upon the man, and when he saw him, his heart was filled with pity. He went over to him, poured oil and wine on his wounds and bandaged them; then he put the man on his own animal and took him to an inn, where he took care of him. The next day he took out two silver coins and gave them to the innkeeper. "Take care of him", he told the innkeeper, "and when I come back this way, I will pay you whatever else you spend on him".'
>
> And Jesus concluded, 'In your opinion, which one of these three acted like a neighbour towards the man attacked by the robbers?'
>
> The teacher of the Law answered, 'The one who was kind to him'.
>
> Jesus replied, 'You go, then, and do the same'.
>
> (Luke 10:25–37 TEV)

Saturday Afternoon at the Footy

'Carn, the Tigers!' Saturday afternoon at the footy, barracking for your team. Panthers, Tigers, Eagles, Bulldogs, Wolves, Magpies, Roosters — names that suggest strength, toughness, ferocity, and an ability to fight. There are chooks that are white and have red combs, but no North Adelaide supporter would want his team to be called the Chooks, or the Hens (although he might call them that when they lose). But he doesn't mind barracking for the Roosters. The rooster struts tall and is the boss of the chook-yard. He can also fight.

You can imagine people's reaction, if we were forming a new club, and, when they asked us what we were going to call ourselves, we said: 'The Lambs'. They'd laugh in our face. 'You can't call yourselves that! Who would ever barrack for the Lambs? "Carn, the mighty Lambs!" It just doesn't work.'

But as Christians that's whom we barrack for — we are people who barrack for the Lamb.

John, the writer of the Book of Revelation, had a vision in which he saw all the inhabitants of heaven gathered in front of God's throne. There in the middle was the Lamb, Jesus. And the enormous crowd of angels, thousands and millions of them, were all applauding and cheering and yelling and shouting. They were singing: 'The Lamb who was killed is worthy to receive power, wealth, wisdom, and strength, honour, glory, and praise!' (Rev. 5:12 TEV).

Then John heard the whole universe joining in, every creature in heaven, on earth, in the world below, and in the sea — all living beings in the universe — and all barracking for the Lamb: 'To him who sits on the throne and to the Lamb, be praise and honour, glory and might, for ever and ever!' (v 13).

Why would anyone want to barrack for the Lamb? It's because this Lamb turned out to be not so weak and helpless as he looked. This Lamb took on all the others — the Panther, the Tiger, the Rooster, the Eagle — and beat the lot. He won. He went top. On the field the Lamb turned out to be a lion.

How did he do it? How could the Lamb beat the Tiger and the Panther?

Football barrackers

We have to understand the particular strength of the Lamb, the particular thing he's good at. The strengths of the Panther and the Tiger are obvious — they have sharp teeth and claws, they are fast and agile, they are strong, and they are ferocious fighters. What does the Lamb have to counter these strengths?

In the summer of 1978–79 a makeshift Australian cricket team was thrashed 5–1 by England in a Test series here in Australia. Afterwards the Australian captain, Graham Yallop, wrote a book called *Lambs to the Slaughter.*

That's what lambs are good at — they are good at getting slaughtered. They are harmless, and easily caught and killed. That's why they've always been one of the main animals used for sacrifices. In biblical times, millions of lambs gave their lives as sacrifices in the temple. At the celebration of the Passover festival, thousands of Passover lambs were slaughtered each year.

This is why God became a Lamb and not a panther or tiger. He became a Lamb so that he could give himself, his life, as a sacrifice to free us from sin. This is what the Lamb was good at — giving his life as a sacrifice for sinners. It was in this strange and unexpected way, by giving his life, that he beat all the others and won.

That's why, in John's vision, the Lamb is cheered as 'the Lamb who was killed'. The terrible wound he carries from the time when he was killed, is not a sign of defeat but of victory.

When Jesus appeared to his disciples after he had been raised to life again, he showed them the terrible wounds in his hands and feet from the crucifixion. He showed these wounds as signs of victory. It was like a retired footballer showing his kids the old scars as proud reminders of past victories. He shows them the scar from the split eyebrow and says: 'That was from the 1972 Grand Final. That was the day we won.'

It used to be said that we were a country that rode on the sheep's back. What was meant was that our wealth and prosperity as a nation depended on sheep.

As Christians, we are people who ride on the sheep's back. We are carried on the back of the Lamb, on Christ's back. He is the one on whom we depend for our real wealth, our eternal prosperity. If we're ever going to get to heaven, it will only be by riding on his back. He's the one who carries us to victory.

It's like the way we're carried to victory on the shoulders of the team we barrack for. When our team wins we say: 'We won, we won!' The players' victory is our victory.

And when your team wins the Grand Final, you celebrate. You go down to the clubrooms, and the players come out on the balcony, and you yell and shout and cheer and sing until you're hoarse.

That's what it's like for us. In barracking for the Lamb we are joining in the great victory celebration that's going on around God's throne in heaven. In the Holy Communion liturgy we sing: 'Therefore with angels and archangels, and with all the company of heaven, we adore and magnify your glorious name'. Earlier in the liturgy we also sing: 'O Lord God, Lamb of God, Son of the Father: You take away the sin of the world; have mercy on us ... For you alone are holy, you alone are Lord, you alone, O Christ, with the Holy Spirit, are most high in the glory of God the Father.' These are victory songs sung in honour of the Lamb, who has won the victory for us over sin and death.

Don't ever be ashamed to be a follower of the Lamb. Keep barracking for him, keep singing your heart out for him. He's the one who carries us to victory.

> Again I looked, and I heard angels, thousands and millions of them! They stood round the throne, the four living creatures, and the elders, and sang in a loud voice:
> 'The Lamb who was killed is worthy
> to receive power, wealth, wisdom, and strength,
> honour, glory, and praise!'
> And I heard every creature in heaven, on earth, in the world below, and in the sea — all living beings in the universe — and they were singing:
> 'To him who sits on the throne and to the Lamb,
> be praise and honour, glory and might,
> for ever and ever!'
> The four living creatures answered, 'Amen!' And the elders fell down and worshipped.
>
> (Revelation 5:11–14 TEV)

The Bushfire

Ivan Southall's novel *Ash Road* is about a devastating bushfire and its consequences for the people living on properties along Ash Road.

87-year-old Grandpa Tanner has stayed behind at his house, and, with everyone else gone, there's no chance any more of getting away. Little Julie, his four-year-old grand-daughter, and also Mrs Robertson's baby, have been left in his care, and now with the fire fast approaching he takes them into the garden to the 44-foot well he dug himself many years ago. He secures the baby in a basket with safety-pins and leather shoe-laces knotted end to end, and lowers it down the well on the end of a clothes line. Then he straps little Julie to a chair, supplies her with lollies and chocolates, and lowers her down the well on another piece of line. In this way he hopes to save the lives of the children, even though he doesn't expect to survive himself.

Julie, of course, isn't very happy slowly turning on the end of a clothes line at the bottom of the well, and Grandpa keeps talking to her to assure her.

> *'I'm staying with you', he called to her. 'I'm here. When the fire's over they'll find Grandpa and then they'll find you. It might take time, little darling; the night might come and the sun might come up again, but they'll find you. Don't cry, or you won't hear them when they come. Shout out loud, won't you? When you hear them come, you sing out: "Here I am, everybody. Down the well, safe and sound".'*
>
> *God was the friend of little children; of that Grandpa was confident. But he dared not ask God to be the friend of an old, old man. Some things were reasonable and some things were not.*

Not long afterwards, with the fire very close now, he covers the well to make it safer for the children.

> *Grandpa Tanner put his pipe down on his tree stump, and poured a bucket of water over himself, and called down the well, 'I'm still here, little darling. Grandpa's going to make it dark now. And remember what Grandpa said. When you hear them come, shout out loud, as loud as you can, "Here I am, everybody. Down the well, safe and sound".' With*

After Ash Wednesday
bushfire

*difficulty, for the wind was troublesome, he slid two sheets
of corrugated iron across the top of the well, and weighted
them down with rocks, and painted on the iron with black
enamel:* Children Here.

*Then he curled up on the leeward side of the stump, drew
a wet woollen blanket over himself, and bit very hard on the
stem of his pipe.*

Finally, with the fire on top of them, there is what the author
calls a 'collision in the sky', and the fire-storm suddenly turns into
a rainstorm. Here are some sections from the last paragraphs of
the book.

*Grandpa Tanner looked out, almost in bewilderment,
from beneath his blanket. Red fire was changing into hissing
steam and frantic billows of smoke. The last flames around
him were leaping and cracking like angry whips, and, having
cracked, they disappeared eerily like genii in an instant.*

He was not to die, not yet ...

Grandpa had not meant the prayer for himself. Surely he had made it clear that it was for Julie and the Robertson baby and for little children everywhere.

But God had sent the rain ...

Grandpa laid his blanket aside. It was ruined. There were dozens of tiny scorch marks on it and several large burns. It had been a good blanket. It was a shame.

Then he pushed the stones away from the sheets of iron with his foot, and a shrill but hollow wail rang from the depths: 'Here I am, everybody. Down the well. Safe and sound.'

This is a story of people whose lives were saved. The lives of little Julie and the Robertson baby were saved by Grandpa lowering them down into the well. Grandpa's life was saved by God sending the rain.

St Paul writes in his letter to Titus about how *our* lives have been saved by God: 'But when the kindness and love of God our Saviour appeared, *he saved us*' (Titus 3:4,5 NIV). St Paul goes on to explain how this has happened.

He saved us, not because of righteous things we had done, but because of his mercy. He saved us through the washing of rebirth and renewal by the Holy Spirit, whom he poured out on us generously through Jesus Christ our Saviour, so that, having been justified by his grace, we might become heirs having the hope of eternal life (vv 5–7).

Our situation was like Grandpa Tanner's. The fire was coming, and there was nothing we could do about it. We were helpless. The situation was hopeless. We were going to die. But in a miraculous way God rescued us. He saved our life.

Grandpa Tanner's life was saved when the rain came pouring down. St Paul says that God has saved us by pouring down on us the water of our baptism, at the same time pouring out his Spirit. It's in our baptism, in that water connected with God's Word, that God has saved us from destruction in the fire.

St Paul says that this pouring out of the Holy Spirit on us in our baptism is done by God 'through Jesus Christ our Saviour'. This means that our baptism is linked with Jesus, with his death for us on the cross and his resurrection. It was on the cross that 'the kindness and love of God our Saviour appeared'. Christian baptism exists because of what Jesus did for us on the cross. In baptism, the Holy Spirit unites us with our crucified and risen Lord, and gives us the blessings won for us by Jesus on the cross.

St Paul tells us what these blessings are. Jesus died on the cross for us, and the Spirit was poured out on us in our baptism, 'so that, having been justified by his grace, we might become heirs having the hope of eternal life'. Everything is now different for us who have been baptized and who belong to Christ. Because of our sin everything was wrong between us and God, and we faced certain death, eternal separation from God. But now, because of Jesus, because of our baptism, we have been brought into a right relationship with God and we have the assurance of eternal life.

St Paul stresses that none of this was our doing; it was all God's doing. Grandpa Tanner contributed nothing to his own rescue. Against all hope and expectation, God had sent the rain. An 87-year-old man could expect no special favours from God, and yet God had shown mercy to him and spared his life.

It's like that for us. 'He saved us, not because of righteous things we had done, but because of his mercy.' If our life has been saved by God, it's not because we have earned it or deserved it. It has come about purely because of the grace and goodness and mercy of God.

We know what the country looks like after a bad bushfire — the trees look dead, everything looks black and ugly and desolate. But when the rains come, we see a transformation take place. The new growth starts to emerge. We see the bush being renewed and regenerated.

Sin is like a bushfire that rages out of control in our life. It makes of our life a blackened, desolate, ugly wasteland. But just as the rain has the power to transform the land, so the water of baptism has the power to transform us. It brings about renewal and regeneration. Baptism is a new birth, it gives us new life — life with God as a member of his family. Our life can now become something green and lush and attractive and useful.

Grandpa Tanner kept reminding Julie what she should say: 'Here I am, everybody. Down the well. Safe and sound.' Through Jesus and his cross, through our baptism, God has rescued us from certain death. He has saved us from the fires of hell. Like Julie we can cry out, with thankfulness to God: 'Here I am, everybody. Down here in the well of my baptism. Here with Jesus. Safe and sound!'

Matthew Flinders and the 'Investigator'

Matthew Flinders has been described as 'among the world's most accomplished navigators and hydrographers, though his exploration was mostly made in unsuitable, leaky or rotten ships'.

One of these leaky, rotten ships was the *Investigator*. She was already an old, decrepit ship when Flinders took command of her and sailed from England in July 1801, to map what was then called 'the Unknown Coast', the southern coast of Australia.

When he arrived in Sydney nine months later, having achieved his aim of mapping the coast of South Australia, the ship was leaking badly. She was overhauled and refitted, and Flinders then sailed north to map sections of the Queensland coast and the northern coast of Australia.

In the Timor Sea the ship began leaking so badly that they beached her for an examination. They discovered she was so rotten that she would founder immediately if caught in a gale and, even if patched up and handled carefully in fine weather, would barely remain afloat for a further six months.

Flinders had to abandon his survey work, but decided to return to Sydney by circumnavigating the continent, something no one had ever done before. He sailed down the west coast, navigated the Bight in the depth of winter, and brought the vessel safely into Port Jackson on June 9, 1803.

Senior naval officers in Sydney inspected the vessel and declared her unseaworthy. They 'ripped off sodden planks, and pushed their canes through her worm-eaten timbers. Her bows were rotten through, the stemson riddled and yellow with decay. The only sound wood was in her stern.' The ship was condemned.

In the sixth month of Elizabeth's pregnancy God sent the angel Gabriel to a town in Galilee named Nazareth. He had a message for a girl promised in marriage to a man named Joseph, who was a descendant of King David. The girl's name was Mary. The angel came to her and said, 'Peace be with you! The Lord is with you and has greatly blessed you!'

Mary was deeply troubled by the angel's message, and she wondered what his words meant. The angel said to her, 'Don't be afraid, Mary; God has been gracious to you. You will become pregnant and give birth to a son, and you will name him Jesus. He will be great and will be called the Son

of the Most High God. The Lord God will make him a king, as
his ancestor David was, and he will be the king of the
descendants of Jacob for ever; his kingdom will never end!'
    Mary said to the angel, 'I am a virgin. How, then, can this
be?'
    The angel answered, 'The Holy Spirit will come on you,
and God's power will rest upon you. For this reason the holy
child will be called the Son of God. Remember your relative
Elizabeth. It is said that she cannot have children, but she
herself is now six months pregnant, even though she is very
old. For there is nothing that God cannot do.'
    'I am the Lord's servant', said Mary; 'may it happen to me
as you have said.' And the angel left her.

(Luke 1:26–38 TEV)

It's amazing that Flinders was able to make such a tremendous
journey — all the way from England and then right round
Australia — in such a poor vessel. But it's even more amazing that
the holy God should have made his tremendous journey to us in
such a poor, weak vessel as Mary.

The *Investigator* is now one of the most famous ships in our
history. But this is not because she was such a marvellous vessel.
She wasn't. She was a leaky, rotten ship, barely fit for use, in the
end a condemned wreck.

Mary is famous among us today, and is given honour and
respect. But this is not because she herself was a specially good or
outstanding person. She wasn't. She was an ordinary, imperfect,
sinful human being like you and me. Like you and me, she was
riddled with sin, like a ship with rotten timbers that's been
condemned.

The *Investigator* is famous, not because she was a good ship,
but because of the man who sailed her and what he achieved. In
the same way, Mary is famous, not because she was a specially
good person, but only because of the One she carried, and
because of the great things he achieved.

God's choice of Mary to be the vessel in which he made that
tremendous voyage to be with us here on earth was an act of
sheer grace and kindness on his part. The angel Gabriel said to
Mary: 'The Lord is with you and has greatly blessed you!' 'Don't
be afraid, Mary; God has been gracious to you' (Luke 1:28,30).

God has been equally gracious to you and me. Christ chooses
to come on board, even though we are rotten through and
through. He doesn't abandon us and leave us to rot. He comes to
us in his Word and in Holy Communion, and joins himself to us.

Through the bread and wine we are able to take his body and blood into our own bodies. By taking command of us, he's able to make something good and useful of us. He gives us a new lease of life.

Flinders had a hard and short life. There were the dangers and hardships of his long voyages. There were times of tragedy, one of them when eight men were drowned off Eyre Peninsula in South Australia at the place he called Cape Catastrophe. On his way back to England, he was unjustly imprisoned by the French Governor of Mauritius for six-and-a-half years. He had been married for three months when he left for Australia in the *Investigator*; he didn't see his bride again for nine years. Back in England, he suffered greatly from ill-health and died at the age of forty.

But his achievements were outstanding. As a result of his work, 'the Unknown Coast' was no longer unknown. His mapping was painstakingly accurate, and it is said that some of his charts of Australian waters are still the best available. His great work, *A Voyage to Terra Australis*, was published the day before he died. The Australian author Geoffrey Dutton has said of him: 'There should be no greater hero for Australians than Flinders'.

The angel Gabriel said to Mary of the child that she would bear: 'He will be great' (Luke 1:32). Jesus' greatness lies in his achievements, in what he achieved for you and me. But these achievements didn't come easily. They came through great suffering and an early death.

The great journey that God made to be with us was a journey that led to the cross. But it was precisely here on the cross that the meaning of the name given to Mary's child was fulfilled. The angel told Mary to call him Jesus, the name which means Saviour, Rescuer, Deliverer. It's through his suffering and death, and through his resurrection from the dead, that Jesus has saved us from the rottenness of sin.

What Jesus has done, through his death and resurrection, is to map the unknown coast for us. He has gone ahead and charted the deep waters for us. He has marked all the rocks and reefs and sandbars, so that they are no longer a danger to us. He saves us from shipwreck. Because of him, we can safely negotiate life's dangerous and difficult waters.

And even when we have to set out for the unknown coast of death, we can do that without fear, because we know that he's been there ahead of us and has charted a safe passage for us.

God chose Mary to be the vessel in which he travelled to earth to be with us and to save us. It was an extraordinary task to which she was called. But God calls us to a similar task. He has chosen you and me to be the vessels by which he can travel to other people in our community.

When we hear this we often respond by pointing out the poor condition we're in: 'Look, all the planks are rotten. I'm not seaworthy. I'm in no fit shape, not equipped for this sort of thing. The best thing for me is to be left in some quiet backwater.'

But that's not Jesus' plan for you and me. He knows that our planks are rotten and that we're nearly falling apart. But he can still use us. He's the expert navigator. He wants to take us out on to the high seas, into uncharted waters. There's still work to be done. There are still people to be found. He wants to use us as the means through which he can come to people with his love, his forgiveness, his grace, his salvation.

And if you think that it can't be done, that it just isn't possible, then you need to hear the promises the angel gives: 'The Holy Spirit will come on you, and God's power will rest upon you.' 'There is nothing that God cannot do' (Luke 1:35,37).

When we hear that promise, and when we remember what great miracles God has already done for us in Jesus, then we will respond in the same trusting and accepting way that Mary did: 'I am the Lord's servant; may it happen to me as you have said' (v 38).

Fleurieu Coast, SA

The Pardoned Convict

The white settlement of Australia began with convicts. In the first few decades after the First Fleet arrived in January 1788, by far the biggest part of the European population consisted of convicts.

The convicts suffered one of the worst fates a person can suffer. Convicted as criminals, often for petty offences, they were then condemned to a life of exile. In being transported halfway round the world to Australia, they were deprived of everything that was dear to them — their home, their land, their families, their rights, their freedom, their future. For many of them it was a sentence of death. Conditions on many of the convict ships were so bad that hundreds died from maltreatment, starvation, and disease.

Many of those who survived the voyage lived and died in this new land as convicts. But others fared better. The various governors of the colony had a policy of pardoning certain convicts and releasing them from their sentence. Convicts released in this way were called emancipists. Many of these emancipated convicts ended up doing quite well for themselves as farmers, traders, manufacturers, and even lawyers and architects.

As Christians, we are like pardoned convicts. A tremendous change has taken place in our life. This has happened as a result of what God has done for us through Jesus.

St Paul writes about this in chapter 5 of his letter to the Romans. He speaks there about the grace of God in which we now live, of how we have been put right with God through faith, and of how we now have peace with God through our Lord Jesus Christ. He also speaks of the hope we now have of sharing God's glory.

In Sydney, in the early years of the colony, the power to release a convict from his sentence lay entirely with the governor. He was the only one who could make this decision, and he could release someone for whatever reason he chose. Sometimes it was done as a reward for industry or good behaviour. At other times it was done simply because people were needed to take up new land.

Whatever the reason, the releasing of a convict from his or her sentence was purely an act of clemency. There was no obligation on the governor to free anyone. The pardoned convict was always the recipient of an act of pure grace on the governor's part.

It's like that for us as Christians. Our pardon lay entirely in God's hands. It was not a reward for good behaviour. As convicts, we had no claim at all on God. Our pardon was an act of pure grace on his part.

St Paul speaks of this when he says that through Jesus 'we have gained access by faith into this grace in which we now stand' (Rom. 5:2 NIV). Previously we stood under God's sentence of condemnation. Now, because of Christ, we stand under his grace and forgiveness.

In the early years of the colony, there was some disagreement among the free settlers as to how far the emancipation of a convict should go, whether or not it should involve a full pardon with the full restoration of civic rights. But from an early time the governors decided that there would be no partial emancipation — it would be all or nothing.

This meant that for a pardoned convict his criminal record was completely removed, and he now enjoyed full legal and political rights. He was still exactly the same person he had been before his pardon, but in the eyes of the law he was now completely different. Instead of being seen as a criminal, he was now regarded and treated as an innocent, upright, law-abiding citizen.

That's how it is for us Christians. For the sake of Jesus, God gives us a full and unconditional pardon. Our sentence is completely wiped out. St Paul refers to this when he speaks of us having been 'justified through faith' (Rom. 5:1). This means that we have been acquitted by God. He pronounces us righteous, he declares us innocent.

Previously I was a convicted criminal. Now I am told: 'You are pardoned. Your sentence is wiped out. I have nothing against you any more.' Previously I was a prisoner. Now I am told: 'You can go free'. I am exactly the same person I was before, and yet in God's eyes I am now completely different. For the sake of Jesus, he no longer regards me as a criminal, but as a good, upright, honest citizen.

Convicts had no real place in society. They were looked down on and despised by everyone. They were seen as enemies of society. The authorities feared and distrusted them, and they feared and distrusted the authorities.

But all this changed for the pardoned convict. He was no longer seen as an enemy of society. He could now take his place in society and begin to relate to people, including the authorities, in new ways.

On one occasion Governor Macquarie invited several pardoned convicts to dinner at Government House to show his full acceptance of them as citizens. As a convict, a man could be flogged for a minor misdemeanour. As a pardoned convict, he could be invited to dinner with the governor.

That's what it's like for us as Christians. When we are set free as a result of Jesus' death for us, our relationship with God undergoes a transformation. St Paul expresses it in this way: 'Since we have been justified through faith, we have peace with God through our Lord Jesus Christ' (Rom. 5:1).

Previously we were at loggerheads with God. We didn't care about him, we were opposed to him. We were his enemies. But Jesus has changed all that. Through his death, he has brought us into a good relationship with God and has made us God's friends. He has made peace between us and God. God now welcomes us in his house and invites us to dinner with him.

The convict was a person without a future. There was really nothing for him to work for or look forward to.

But things were quite different when he was set free. Sometimes he was given land. He now had a personal investment in the country and its future. He could start to think about a future for himself and his family. He had some real incentive to work and to achieve something.

There would have still been great difficulties and hardships, of course. He might very well have worked harder now than as a convict, when he bludged whenever he could. He had more worries and responsibilities now that he was working for himself. But he put up with the hardships without grizzling because he was free now, and he had something to work for and to look forward to.

It's like that for us as Christians. Because of what Jesus has done for us, we have a future, we have lots to look forward to. St Paul refers to this future as our 'hope'. He says: 'And we rejoice in the hope of the glory of God' (Rom. 5:2).

We know that in the meantime there will be hardships and difficulties. As Christians, we have to expect opposition and suffering. But we put up with these things gladly. They simply strengthen our resolve to hold on to what we have in Christ, and they make us look forward more eagerly to the good things ahead of us. St Paul puts it this way: 'We also rejoice in our sufferings, because we know that suffering produces perseverance; perseverance, character; and character, hope' (Rom. 5:3,4).

This hope, St Paul adds, is not a false hope. The future we look forward to is something sure and certain. This certainty comes from the Holy Spirit's presence with us. St Paul says: 'Hope does not disappoint us, because God has poured out his love into our hearts by the Holy Spirit, whom he has given us' (Rom. 5:5).

The Holy Spirit makes us certain of our future by pouring God's love into our hearts, that is, by making us certain of God's love for us in Jesus. Where we have in our hearts this certainty of God's love for us, we can also be sure of the great future God has in store for us.

In speaking of the pardon we convicts have received from God, St Paul mentions the role played by all three members of the Holy Trinity — the Father, the Son Jesus Christ, and the Holy Spirit.

We could describe the Holy Trinity as 'The Royal Society for the Emancipation and Rehabilitation of Convicts'. This is what God has worked so hard for — to set us free and give us a new life. We are the beneficiaries of the marvellous work of this society.

> *Therefore, since we have been justified through faith, we have peace with God through our Lord Jesus Christ, through whom we have gained access by faith into this grace in which we now stand. And we rejoice in the hope of the glory of God. Not only so, but we also rejoice in our sufferings, because we know that suffering produces perseverance; perseverance, character; and character, hope. And hope does not disappoint us, because God has poured out his love into our hearts by the Holy Spirit, whom he has given us.*
>
> (Romans 5:1–5 NIV).

Sunrise in Central Australia

There was a time, while we were living at Hermannsburg in central Australia, when I was training to run in the Alice Springs marathon. In the winter months I was getting up before daybreak, and I would set off on my run when there was just enough light to see the potholes in the dirt road. It would be freezing cold, and I'd have my old jumper on, a beanie over my ears, and gloves on my hands.

I would head out of Hermannsburg due east along the Alice Springs road. And there were times when the morning star, the planet Venus, would be up in the sky straight ahead of me, heralding the new day. In the clear, dry, central Australian atmosphere, this planet, the brightest of all the stars, would stand out in the sky really big and bright.

As the day dawned and the light became brighter, the stars would begin to fade and disappear from the sky. The morning star was the last to disappear. I was often surprised at how long it remained visible. Sometimes I could still see it, even though the sky had become quite bright — but only because I knew exactly where to look for it.

But when the sun finally broke over the horizon through the mulga trees, then the morning star had no chance of competing any more. Together with all the other stars it became invisible.

All those stars that had shone so brightly in the clear night sky only a short time before, could now no longer be seen. It often struck me that it wasn't that they weren't there any more — they were all still there, still shining up in the sky. But they couldn't be seen any more — not because it was too dark, or because something was blocking the light from reaching the earth. The reason was that the sky was too light, too bright. The light of the stars was eclipsed by the light of the sun. The light of the sun was so much greater, so much more powerful, that it completely swallowed up the light from the stars, including the light of the morning star.

John the Baptist was God's messenger sent to prepare the way for Jesus. He 'came to tell people about the light, so that all should hear the message and believe. He himself was not the light; he came to tell about the light' (John 1:7,8 TEV).

John was like the morning star preparing the way for Jesus, whose coming was like the rising of the sun. Just as the morning star in the east heralds the dawning of the new day, so John came to herald the new day that has come for us with the coming of Jesus.

John came as a bright light, the brightest star in the sky at that time. And people began asking, is this the Messiah? Is this the beginning of the new day we've been waiting for?

But John kept repeating and stressing that he was not the Messiah. He was only the messenger, the herald, the servant. He was only the voice shouting in the desert, getting the way ready for the greater one who was coming.

John insisted that the one coming after him was so much greater than he was: 'I am not good enough even to untie his sandals' (Luke 1:27). It would be like the light of the sun in comparison to the light of the morning star. The light of Jesus is so bright that it eclipses all other light. In the brightness of this sun, the light from all the stars and planets is swallowed up.

With the coming of Jesus the sun has risen, and a new day has dawned for us.

What is it that makes the light of Jesus so much brighter than any other light? What is it that makes him so great that even a great man like John pales into insignificance beside him, is not worthy to even untie his sandals?

Jesus' greatness does not lie in his coming with great pomp and ceremony, with great and flashy displays of power. On the contrary, he comes in humility and weakness as a baby born in a stable. People didn't even recognize him. John told the people that Jesus stood among them as the one they did not know.

We know now that our own sun is not a particularly big star. In fact, it's one of the smaller stars in our galaxy and in the universe as a whole. It seems so big to us in comparison to other stars only because it's so close.

Jesus didn't come to us as the greatest sun in the universe. He made himself small. His greatness lies in the fact that he came close to us.

John the Baptist pointed to Jesus and said: 'There is the Lamb of God, who takes away the sin of the world!' (John 1:29 TEV). Jesus comes to give himself as a sacrifice for us on the cross. This is his greatness. It is the greatness of his self-giving and self-sacrificing love.

Sunrise

The light, that tremendous energy that comes to us from the sun, is generated by the sun burning itself up. Eventually the sun will have used up all its fuel, and it will die.

The great light that comes to us from Jesus comes from his giving of himself for us, his readiness to die for us. The light that he brings is the tremendous energy of his love which we see released for us on the cross and in his resurrection. It's this self-giving love of Jesus for us that makes his light so bright, that makes him so much greater than anyone else.

The first thing God said when he created the world was: 'Let there be light' (Gen. 1:3). This world, this universe began with the creation of light. Without light there couldn't be life and we wouldn't be here.

The coming of John the Baptist announces that God's new act of creation is about to occur. A new beginning for this world, this universe, is about to take place. The sun is about to come up on a new day for humankind.

This new day, this new creation, has come for us with the coming of Jesus. Through his birth, death, and resurrection he has dispelled the darkness of sin and death. A wonderful, bright, new light has begun to shine on us.

Now we are people who have the opportunity to live in the light of God's new day. This means not only continuing to receive the light that comes from Christ in his Word and in his Supper, but also letting his light reflect from us to others.

The light of the sun reflects from the planet Venus and makes it shine as the brightest star in the sky. In the same way, that bright and burning love of Jesus is to reflect from us, bringing his love and his life to people who are still in the dark. The energy of Christ's love can make us energetic in showing love and care to the people around us.

St Paul, in his Letter to the Philippians, tells us to

'be innocent and pure as God's perfect children, who live in a world of corrupt and sinful people. You must shine among them like stars lighting up the sky, as you offer them the message of life' (Phil. 2:15,16 TEV).

Live in the wonderful light of Christ, and reflect his light to others.

God sent his messenger, a man named John, who came to tell people about the light, so that all should hear the message and believe. He himself was not the light; he came to tell about the light . . .

The Jewish authorities in Jerusalem sent some priests and Levites to John, to ask him, 'Who are you?'

John did not refuse to answer, but spoke out openly and clearly, saying: 'I am not the Messiah'.

'Who are you, then?' they asked. 'Are you Elijah?'

'No, I am not', John answered.

'Are you the Prophet?' they asked.

'No', he replied.

'Then tell us who you are', they said. 'We have to take an answer back to those who sent us. What do you say about yourself?'

John answered by quoting the prophet Isaiah:

' "I am the voice of someone shouting
*   in the desert:*
Make a straight path for the Lord to
*   travel!" '*

The messengers, who had been sent by the Pharisees, then asked John, 'If you are not the Messiah nor Elijah nor the Prophet, why do you baptize?'

John answered, 'I baptize with water, but among you stands the one you do not know. He is coming after me, but I am not good enough even to untie his sandals.'

All this happened in Bethany on the east side of the River Jordan, where John was baptizing.

(John 1:6–8, 19–28 TEV)

Peter Lalor and the Eureka Stockade

Jesus told a parable about the final judgment, in which he said that when he returns, everyone will be gathered before him and he will divide them into two groups, with the righteous people on his right and the others on his left.

He will say to the people on his right: 'Come, you who are blessed by my Father; take your inheritance, the kingdom prepared for you since the creation of the world. For I was hungry and you gave me something to eat, I was thirsty and you gave me something to drink, I was a stranger and you invited me in, I needed clothes and you clothed me, I was sick and you looked after me, I was in prison and you came to visit me' (Matt. 25:34–36 NIV).

The righteous will be completely mystified by this, and will ask when they did any of these things for him. He will answer: 'I tell you the truth, whatever you did for one of the least of these brothers of mine, you did for me' (v 40).

A glass of water for someone who's thirsty — what's so special about that? Why should my eternal destiny hang on something so simple and ordinary? Wouldn't all of us give a drink to someone who was thirsty?

Not necessarily. There could be times when we would not give a drink to someone who needed one. We might not want to be seen associating with that person. We might not want to appear to be on his side. It might be too dangerous.

Peter Lalor became the leader of the miners at the Eureka Stockade in Ballarat when, in 1854, they took up arms to protect themselves against the licence-hunting raids of the authorities.

When the troops attacked and over-ran the stockade before dawn on Sunday December 3, Lalor's left shoulder was shattered in the first volley of shots from the soldiers. A fellow digger hid him in a hollow covered over with slabs just outside the stockade, and in this way he escaped the soldiers' bayonets. While he was hidden there, another friend brought him some wine to drink. During the rest of that day, and in the days that followed, Lalor was kept hidden and was cared for by various people.

These people gave help to Peter Lalor when his life depended on it. They gave him food and drink. They took him into their homes. They cared for him while he was desperately ill. They clothed him.

In doing all this they were putting themselves at grave risk. They were showing themselves prepared to associate with the rebels. Thirteen men had already been arrested and charged with high treason, for which they could hang if found guilty. On the poster offering a reward of £200 for information about Lalor, the accusation was that he did 'use certain treasonable and seditious language, and incite men to take up arms, with a view to make war against Our Sovereign Lady the Queen'.

It's one thing to offer a beer or a cuppa to a friend. It's another thing altogether to give a drink to a man who is wanted by the authorities and is accused of serious crimes. You could get into serious trouble by appearing to be on his side.

On that Friday morning when a man called Jesus was led out of Jerusalem to be executed as a criminal on a charge of having tried to lead a revolt, who of us would have been prepared to step forward to give him aid? When he cried out from the cross 'I'm thirsty', would any of us have been prepared to give this condemned man a drink? None of his followers were there. None of them wanted to risk being linked with this man. Peter was prepared to swear black and blue that he didn't even know the man.

That was a long time ago. We have the perfect alibi — we weren't there. But that still doesn't let us off the hook, because in his parable Jesus says he is still present among us here today. He is present among us in people still needing help and support and comfort and care. He says: 'Whatever you did for one of the least of these brothers of mine, you did for me.'

Who are these brothers and sisters in Jesus? Perhaps they are any person in need of my help. But those who are brothers and sisters of Jesus in a special way are those who belong to him as his followers. These are the ones with whom he identifies himself. They are his body. We who follow Jesus as our Lord are his brothers and sisters.

In the early days of the Church, and in all the centuries since then, the followers of Christ have often been persecuted. Will you visit the followers of Christ when they are being thrown into prison? Will you be prepared to identify with your fellow-Christians when they are being mistreated and are in need of clothing and shelter, food and drink?

Or today, here in Australia, when Christianity is seen as old-fashioned, out-dated, and irrelevant, and when Christians are mocked for being sissy, superstitious, or hopelessly misguided, are you prepared to associate with fellow Christians, to identify with them, to show that you belong to them by helping and caring for them, supporting and encouraging them?

This is the basis, Jesus says, on which we will be judged. Sometimes the judgment of history on people is different from the way they were judged in their own lifetime. The men of the Eureka Stockade were judged as dangerous revolutionaries by the authorities of their own day. Today they are more likely to be seen as heroes, men of courage who did the right thing in opposing injustice.

The important thing for us is not how we will be judged by history, but how we will be judged by God. God's judgment on people will often be quite different from the way they were judged by other people. What will be Jesus' judgment on us when he returns? Will the verdict be eternal punishment, or eternal life?

The basis for judgment is clear. When everyone else was against him, were we prepared to identify with the crucified Christ and his persecuted and ridiculed brothers and sisters? Have we shown care and concern and compassion for Christ by showing care and concern and compassion for one another? Whose side are we on? This is the key question by which we will be judged by Christ.

The miners who made their stand at the Eureka Stockade did so under a special flag designed by one of their men, a man called Charles Ross. They called the flag the Southern Cross. It consisted of a white cross on a dark blue background, with a star in the centre of the cross and a star at the end of each of the four arms of the cross.

When the flag was raised, five hundred diggers knelt around the pole. Peter Lalor raised his right hand and said: 'We swear by the Southern Cross to stand truly by each other, and fight to defend our rights and liberties'. The others all raised their right hands too and said: 'Amen!'

We will be able to stand in the judgment on the last day as those who have taken their stand under the cross of Christ. In our baptism we have received the sign of the holy cross. Christ has taken us to be his, and we have taken our stand under his flag.

To live under the cross means living as a person committed to Christ, who gave himself on the cross for me. It means that I am not ashamed to belong to the crucified one. It means that I live my life looking to him and his cross for forgiveness and the power to begin a new life.

And to live under the cross also means living as people committed to each other, as those who have sworn to stand truly by each other and not let each other down. It means that I am not frightened or ashamed to stand by my fellow Christian when everyone else is against him or her. It means that, just as Jesus gave himself on the cross for us, so we keep learning from him how to give ourselves to one another in showing care and compassion, in giving comfort and encouragement.

Stick your neck out — give a drink to your brother who needs help and support. Take a risk — share your food with the person shunned by everyone else. Do it for Christ's sake. Remember that he stuck his neck out and risked everything for you.

Don't do it for hope of reward. Do it simply out of happiness and gratitude for what Jesus did for you, and out of genuine care and concern for your brother or sister who needs help.

Show whose side you're on. Take your stand under Christ's flag. Live your life under the cross.

> 'When the Son of Man comes in his glory, and all the angels with him, he will sit on his throne in heavenly glory. All the nations will be gathered before him, and he will separate the people one from another as a shepherd separates the sheep from the goats. He will put the sheep on his right and the goats on his left.
>
> 'Then the King will say to those on his right, "Come, you who are blessed by my Father; take your inheritance, the kingdom prepared for you since the creation of the world. For I was hungry and you gave me something to eat, I was thirsty and you gave me something to drink, I was a stranger and you invited me in, I needed clothes and you clothed me, I was sick and you looked after me, I was in prison and you came to visit me."
>
> 'Then the righteous will answer him, "Lord, when did we see you hungry and feed you, or thirsty and give you something to drink? When did we see you a stranger and invite you in, or needing clothes and clothe you? When did we see you sick or in prison and go to visit you?"
>
> 'The King will reply, "I tell you the truth, whatever you did for one of the least of these brothers of mine, you did for me".

'Then he will say to those on his left, "Depart from me, you who are cursed, into the eternal fire prepared for the devil and his angels. For I was hungry and you gave me nothing to eat, I was thirsty and you gave me nothing to drink, I was a stranger and you did not invite me in. I needed clothes and you did not clothe me, I was sick and in prison and you did not look after me."

'They also will answer, "Lord, when did we see you hungry or thirsty or a stranger or needing clothes or sick or in prison, and did not help you?"

'He will reply, "I tell you the truth, whatever you did not do for one of the least of these, you did not do for me".

'Then they will go away to eternal punishment, but the righteous to eternal life.'

(Matthew 25:31–46 NIV)

Sovereign Hill, Vic.

Ayers Rock

The Aborigines call it Uluru. White Australians call it Ayers Rock. To Territorians it's simply The Rock.

I'll never forget my first visit to Ayers Rock. It came after we'd already been living in central Australia for eight years. I hadn't been in any particular hurry to see it. I'd seen so many pictures of it that I reckoned I already knew what it looked like, and my expectations weren't very great.

It knocked me off my feet. None of the pictures had been able to convey its sheer size. There it stood, out in the desert in the flat sandhill country, enormous, strong, solid, awe-inspiring, impressive.

The Rock is of great significance to the Aborigines of that area. Especially in the early days before white settlement, the big rock-pools at its base were an important source of water. The place is also of great religious significance, with many sacred stories, songs, and ceremonies associated with the caves and other features of the rock. For the Aborigines the Rock has been a place that has provided both physical and spiritual security.

There was an occasion when Jesus spoke of Peter as a rock. It happened after Jesus had asked the disciples: 'Who do people say the Son of Man is?' They had answered: 'Some say John the Baptist; others say Elijah; and still others, Jeremiah or one of the prophets'. Jesus had then asked them: 'But what about you? Who do you say I am?' Peter, speaking for all of them, had answered: 'You are the Christ, the Son of the living God'.

Jesus then said to Peter: 'Blessed are you, Simon son of Jonah, for this was not revealed to you by man, but by my Father in heaven'. Then he added: 'And I tell you that you are Peter, and on this rock I will build my church, and the gates of Hades will not overcome it' (Matt. 16:13–18 NIV).

Jesus said that he was going to build his church on a rock, and that rock would be Peter. Peter the rock? Peter the pebble, more like it, or Peter the sandhill! We know what Peter was like — strong in some ways, but pitifully weak in others; impetuous and well-meaning, but completely unreliable; quick to say that he was ready to die for his Lord, but just as quick to disown him at

Ayers Rock, NT

the first sign of danger. How could Jesus hope to build a strong and secure church on someone so weak and unreliable?

If Peter and the other apostles are the Ayers Rock of the church, this is not because they are strong or great, but because they have a special role to play. They are the foundation of the church because they are the first ones to discover who Jesus really is, and the first ones to start telling others about him.

It's because of their faith in Jesus and their witness to him that we, and many others through the ages, have been able to know Jesus and come to faith in him. Without the message that has come down to us from the apostles in the preaching of the church and in the Bible, the church would not exist, and we ourselves would not belong to Christ today.

Peter and the apostles tower over the rest of us, like Ayers Rock over the surrounding countryside, only because they occupy this unique position as the first witnesses to Christ. In every other respect, they were ordinary, weak, sinful human beings like you and me. If they are the rock foundation for the church, it is only because God himself chose them for this task and equipped them for it.

Jesus made it clear that Peter's great confession of faith in him was not something for which Peter himself could take credit. He said to Peter: 'This was not revealed to you by man, but by my Father in heaven'. God himself is the one who gives faith, and he is the one who also created the faith of the apostles. He is the one who has made them the rock for the church.

Immediately after Peter's confession of faith in Jesus, Jesus 'warned his disciples not to tell anyone that he was the Christ' (Matt. 16:20). He did this because his work as the Messiah was not yet finished. It was only after his work of dying on the cross for us had taken place, that the apostles themselves could fully understand who he was and what he had come to do, and could then start telling others about him. They were the unique eye-witnesses of Jesus' death and resurrection, and that's why they have a unique place as the foundation on which the church is built.

Jesus told Peter and the others: 'I will give you the keys of the kingdom of heaven; whatever you bind on earth will be bound in heaven, and whatever you loose on earth will be loosed in heaven' (v 19). He gave them the power to either permit or prohibit a person's entry into God's Kingdom. This is a power they exercised by proclaiming the crucified and risen Christ as the only one who can free us from our sin and gain entry to heaven for us.

This work, begun by the apostles, has continued through the ages, and is still carried on today. It takes place in the church, and this is why the existence of the church is so crucial for us. The church is the place where the witness of the apostles continues. This is where sins are forgiven in the name of Jesus, where Jesus is made present for us — in the preached Word, in Baptism, and in Holy Communion — as the Messiah, as our Saviour from sin, and where the door to heaven is opened for us.

It's easy to rubbish the church and dismiss it as a mob of weak, sinful people who don't seem to amount to much. But Jesus assures us that this church rests on solid rock. This rock is the apostles and their message, their faith and witness to Jesus Christ and his death and resurrection.

Don't base your life on the shifting and insecure sandhills of the desert. Stay with the rock. Stay with the church. It mightn't look much, but it's more solid than Ayers Rock. This is where there is real security, because this is where Jesus is found. This rock is so strong that even 'the gates of Hades will not overcome it'.

When Jesus came to the region of Caesarea Philippi, he asked his disciples, 'Who do people say the Son of Man is?'

They replied, 'Some say John the Baptist; others say Elijah; and still others, Jeremiah or one of the prophets'.

'But what about you?' he asked. 'Who do you say I am?'

Simon Peter answered, 'You are the Christ, the Son of the living God'.

Jesus replied, 'Blessed are you, Simon son of Jonah, for this was not revealed to you by man, but by my Father in heaven. And I tell you that you are Peter, and on this rock I will build my church, and the gates of Hades will not overcome it. I will give you the keys of the kingdom of heaven; whatever you bind on earth will be bound in heaven, and whatever you loose on earth will be loosed in heaven.' Then he warned his disciples not to tell anyone that he was the Christ.

(Matthew 16:13–20)

The Man from Snowy River

> There was movement at the station, for the word had passed
> around
> That the colt from old Regret had got away,
> And had joined the wild bush horses — he was worth a
> thousand pound,
> So all the cracks had gathered to the fray.

This is the beginning of Banjo Paterson's famous poem *The Man from Snowy River*. It tells the story of the crack riders who gathered at the homestead to run down the mob of wild horses and get back the prize colt that had got away and joined them.

Among the riders, there's a young man on 'a small and weedy beast'. The boss tells him: 'Lad, you'd better stop away, those hills are far too rough for such as you'. But Clancy of the Overflow puts in a good word for him, and in the end he's allowed to come.

You know the rest — how the man from Snowy River does what none of the other crack riders could do, how he follows the mob down the mountainside where none of the others dare to go, and how finally, 'alone and unassisted', he brings the mob back.

What we like about this story is that it's the underdog, the one who was originally rejected as not being good enough to come, who in the end achieves what none of the others could do. Those who fancied themselves turned out to be failures. And the one who was rejected and looked least likely to succeed turns out to be the best.

In a famous passage in the Bible, the prophet Isaiah speaks of a man who was despised and rejected. This person seemed to have absolutely nothing going for him. There was nothing about him to suggest that he could achieve anything. 'He had no dignity or beauty to make us take notice of him. There was nothing attractive about him, nothing that would draw us to him. We despised him and rejected him' (Isa. 53:2,3 TEV). He was a complete outcast, a complete reject.

But the astonishing thing is that this man whose whole life seemed to be nothing but shame, defeat, suffering, and failure, is seen in the end to have done something that no one else was able to do. This reject, this outcast, turns out to be the deliverer of his people. The one who was treated brutally and with contempt is the one who is finally honoured by God and gazed at in wonder by kings.

What this is telling us is that if we are to find the champion sent by God to rescue us, then it's no good looking among the crack riders — the powerful, the clever, those who are successful and admired by all. Instead, we are directed to a man hanging on a cross, wounded, beaten up, shockingly disfigured, a man led off like a lamb to the slaughter, weak, defenceless, treated with contempt. 'Many people were shocked when they saw him; he was so disfigured that he hardly looked human' (Isa. 52:14). But the astonishing thing is that it's through this man, through this suffering servant of God who was despised and rejected, that God achieves his plan for us. God says: 'My servant will succeed in his task'. 'Through him my purposes will succeed' (Isa. 52:13; 53:10). It's through Jesus and his cross that we are rescued by God.

The men who looked down on the man from Snowy River and wanted him excluded from the ride would have felt pretty silly afterwards. They would have to admit that they were completely wrong — wrong about him, because he turned out to be much better than they thought, and wrong about themselves, because it turned out that they weren't as good as they thought they were.

This is what happens when we see what Jesus did for us on the cross. We are forced to admit that we have been wrong — wrong about this man whom we despised and rejected, and wrong in our ideas about how good we were.

The people who despised and rejected the Lord's servant thought that his suffering was proof that *he* was in the wrong, that he was guilty and was being punished by God. 'All the while we thought that his suffering was punishment sent by God' (Isa. 53:4). But now they can see that *they* were the ones in the wrong. 'But because of our sins he was wounded, beaten because of the evil we did' (v 5). They now have a keen sense of their own failure. 'All of us were like sheep that were lost, each of us going his own way. But the Lord made the punishment fall on him, the punishment all of us deserved' (v 6).

When we look to the cross we see that Jesus has gone where none of us was able to go, and has achieved something that none of us could ever have done. This weedy, insignificant rider shows us up. He shows that we are not as good as we thought we were. Only at the cross can we start to see ourselves as we really are.

Only here can we start to see how stupid, ignorant, blind, and wrong we have been.

When the man from Snowy River brought the horses back, the other riders could only look on with astonished admiration. They didn't hold back in their praise of what he'd done; it was an incredible achievement. They had to hand it to him — where they had failed as a group, he had succeeded on his own. They would have given him the honour and respect due to him. The poem concludes: 'The Man from Snowy River is a household word today, and the stockmen tell the story of his ride'.

What makes his achievement all the more praiseworthy is that it was done as a favour for someone else — it wasn't his own horse he was retrieving. For the sake of someone else he was prepared to risk his life. It was a hard thing to do. We're not told what he himself felt like at the end of the ride, but we're told that his pony 'could scarcely raise a trot', and 'was blood from hip to shoulder from the spur'.

What Jesus did on the cross was not done for himself. It was done for the sake of others. It was done for you and me. 'He endured the suffering that should have been ours, the pain that we should have borne.' 'Because of our sins he was wounded, beaten because of the evil we did' (Isa. 53:4,5). All this happened for *our* benefit. 'We are healed by the punishment he suffered, made whole by the blows he received' (v 5). God says of him: 'My devoted servant with whom I am pleased, will bear the punishment of many and for his sake I will forgive them' (v 11).

It wasn't an easy thing to do. He ended up giving his life for us. When we see him there on the cross, blood from head to foot, we can begin to understand the courage and the strength and the love for us that were needed to carry the task through. It was an incredible achievement.

That's why we can't look at the cross of Jesus without being filled with astonished admiration. We have to hand it to him. He deserves all the praise we can give him. We have to give him the honour and respect due to him. This is why the name of Jesus is a household word among us today, and why we keep on telling and retelling to whomever will listen the story of what he did for us on the cross.

If you look to the cross of Christ you will see a man hanging there, bloody, beaten, broken. Don't be put off by what you see. Don't be ashamed to belong to this crucified one. This despised and rejected man is a champion — our champion. He went where we couldn't go and did what we couldn't do. He went looking for us when we were lost, and brought us safely back to God. This reject is our Saviour.

> The Lord says,
> 'My servant will succeed in his task;
>   he will be highly honoured.
> Many people were shocked when they saw him;
>   he was so disfigured that he hardly looked human.
> But now many nations will marvel at him,
>   and kings will be speechless with amazement.
> They will see and understand
>   something they had never known.'
>   The people reply,
>   'Who would have believed what we now report?
>   Who could have seen the Lord's hand in this?
> It was the will of the Lord that his servant
>   should grow like a plant taking root in dry ground.
> He had no dignity or beauty
>   to make us take notice of him.
> There was nothing attractive about him,
>   nothing that would draw us to him.
> We despised him and rejected him;
>   he endured suffering and pain.
> No one would even look at him —
>   we ignored him as if he were nothing
>
> 'But he endured the suffering that should have been ours,
>   the pain that we should have borne.
> All the while we thought that his suffering
>   was punishment sent by God.
> But because of our sins he was wounded,
>   beaten because of the evil we did.
> We are healed by the punishment he suffered,
>   made whole by the blows he received.
> All of us were like sheep that were lost,
>   each of us going his own way.
> But the Lord made the punishment fall on him,
>   the punishment all of us deserved.
>
> 'He was treated harshly, but endured it humbly;
>   he never said a word.
> Like a lamb about to be slaughtered,
> like a sheep about to be sheared,
>   he never said a word.
> He was arrested and sentenced and led off to die,
>   and no one cared about his fate.

He was put to death for the sins of our people.
He was placed in a grave with evil men,
*   he was buried with the rich,*
even though he had never committed a crime
*   or ever told a lie.'*
*   The Lord says,*
'It was my will that he should suffer;
*   his death was a sacrifice to bring forgiveness.*
And so he will see his descendants;
*   he will live a long life,*
*   and through him my purpose will succeed.*
After a life of suffering, he will again have joy;
*   he will know that he did not suffer in vain.*
My devoted servant, with whom I am pleased,
*   will bear the punishment of many*
*   and for his sake I will forgive them.*
And so I will give him a place of honour,
*   a place among great and powerful men.*
He willingly gave his life
*   and shared the fate of evil men.*
He took the place of many sinners
*   and prayed that they might be forgiven.'*
                                    (Isaiah 52:13–53:12 TEV)

The Outback Missionary

Pastor Carl Strehlow was the missionary at Hermannsburg in central Australia for 28 years, from 1894 to 1922. During this time, his achievements as a student of Aboriginal language and culture, as translator, preacher and teacher, and as mission administrator were outstanding.

He died prematurely at the age of 52, while attempting a journey south from Hermannsburg to the railhead at Oodnadatta to get medical aid. He was suffering from pleurisy and dropsy, an extremely painful condition in which fluid collects in the lower part of the body. After an agonizing journey by horse and buggy through rough country, he died at a place called Horseshoe Bend on the Finke River. He lies buried there in a lonely outback grave, in a coffin made from whisky cases.

Carl Strehlow had always been a strong man — strong-willed and strong of faith. He had left his homeland and devoted his life whole-heartedly to mission work among the Aboriginals. Some months earlier, before he had become sick, Strehlow had silenced the doubts expressed by his wife about their uncertain future by assuring her that if they had complete faith in God he would — in fact must — answer their prayers. He added that if God did not keep his promises, they would have the right to throw the Bible down at his feet.

A few months later, on that painful journey down the Finke River, he is said at one stage to have picked up his Bible, looked at it for some time, and then hurled it into the bush.

Not only was he suffering physical agony, but he was also undergoing an intense spiritual struggle. He was overcome by the sense of having been abandoned by God, by God's seeming lack of compassion, and by the wall of silence that met all his prayers. After serving God so faithfully, he seemed to be abandoned out here in the lonely desert, to die a painful death.

John the Baptist was a strong man too, a man on fire for God and with a fiery message on his lips. Here was another man who had given up the easy and comfortable life to go into the desert and devote his whole life to the service of God. He was no weakling, no mere blade of grass bending in the wind. He was no softie, dressed up in fancy clothes and living in luxury in a palace. He was a strong and tough man, unafraid to proclaim God's

The Strehlow family and Aboriginal friends, Hermannsburg, NT, about 1917

message in all its uncompromising harshness even to the religious leaders and political rulers of his time.

But now he was languishing in prison, put there by King Herod, whom he had offended. He knew that he could be killed at any time, and that his life's work was probably coming to a premature end.

It was at this time that he sent some of his followers with a question for Jesus. They asked him: 'Are you the one who was to come, or should we expect someone else?'

We catch a glimpse here of John, in his suffering and in the face of a violent and premature death, struggling with his faith. He had announced the coming of the Messiah, and had welcomed him in the person of Jesus of Nazareth. Now he is asking himself: 'Is it true? Have I been deluded, and have I been leading others into error? If this man really is the Messiah, where is the evidence? Why do tyranny and injustice still flourish? Why must I suffer like this?'

It can be disturbing, even shocking, to see great men and women of God experiencing doubts, struggling with their faith. If their strong faith is shaken, what of my weak faith?

But they are human beings like you and me, and in the face of hardship and suffering they experience the same doubts, fears, and questionings that all of us go through.

Carl Strehlow, in his own suffering, reflected on the fact that it was 'the finest and best men and women in the community, and those who had loved God and trusted him beyond everything, who sometimes were subjected to the most cruel experiences possible'. He also remembered that Jesus himself, with the time of his crucifixion very close, underwent an exhausting struggle in the Garden of Gethsemane in learning to submit his will to that of his Father.

It is not an unusual or shameful thing to struggle with doubts. Jesus is not offended by our questioning. Faith is a precious gift of God, but there are times when it also becomes a fearful struggle.

Jesus gave an answer to John's question. He said:

> Go back and report to John what you hear and see: The blind receive sight, the lame walk, those who have leprosy are cured, the deaf hear, the dead are raised, and the good news is preached to the poor (Matt. 11:4,5 NIV).

These are the signs that the promises and prophecies are coming true, that the Messiah has come, that the kingdom of God is breaking in on this world of sin, sickness, and death.

Here is the evidence that John was looking for. But this evidence doesn't do away with the need for faith. John saw none of this evidence in his own situation. The presence of the Messiah did not bring about his release from prison or put an end to his sufferings. It didn't stop him from soon having his head cut off.

Jesus' reply to John is really an encouragement to believe, an encouragement to trust. Jesus is saying to John: 'Trust me. Don't lose faith in me. Believe me that I am the Messiah, the promised Saviour sent by God.'

There are times when we too are in distress, and cannot see any evidence of God's goodness. All we can do then is to hold on to Jesus' words and look at what he has done. His words and actions are an encouragement for us to believe, in spite of all appearances, that he is the fulfilment of all God's promises, that he is the one sent by God to save and to heal. Jesus says: 'Blessed is the man who does not fall away on account of me' (Matt. 11:6).

Jesus was not shocked by John's doubts, nor was he in any way critical of him. On the contrary, he said that, in spite of his doubts, 'there has not risen anyone greater than John the Baptist'. At the same time he added: 'Yet he who is least in the kingdom of heaven is greater than he' (v 11).

If you and I are greater than John, this is not because we have a stronger faith than he, or because we have no doubts. Our faith is not always strong, and being in God's kingdom does not spare us from doubts.

If we are greater than John it is only because we are united in a special way with the one who is greater than John — with Jesus. John didn't live to see Jesus' greatest miracle, the one that all the others were pointing to — his death for us on the cross. Through our Christian baptism, we have been united with Jesus and with his death and resurrection. We have been healed by him and made whole. We are greater than John simply because of the greater miracles that have been performed for us by Jesus.

As a human being like you and me, Jesus also had doubts and struggled with his faith. He knew the feeling of being abandoned by God when he cried out, in his agony on the cross: 'My God, my God, why did you abandon me?' (Matt. 27:46 TEV)

He is with us in our doubts and in our struggles of faith. He is there with us in the shocks and traumas of life. He is there as the one who brings healing and hope. He's the one we can keep hanging on to when everything else is gone.

> When John heard in prison what Christ was doing, he sent his disciples to ask Jesus, 'Are you the one who was to come, or should we expect someone else?'
>
> Jesus replied, 'Go back and report to John what you hear and see: The blind receive sight, the lame walk, those who have leprosy are cured, the deaf hear, the dead are raised, and the good news is preached to the poor. Blessed is the man who does not fall away on account of me.'
>
> As John's disciples were leaving, Jesus began to speak to the crowd about John:
>
> 'What did you go out into the desert to see? A reed swayed by the wind? If not, what did you go out to see? A man dressed in fine clothes? No, those who wear fine clothes are in kings' palaces. Then what did you go out to see? A prophet? Yes, I tell you, and more than a prophet. This is the one about whom it is written:
>
> "I will send my messenger ahead of you,
> who will prepare your way before you".
>
> I tell you the truth: Among those born of women there has not risen anyone greater than John the Baptist; yet he who is least in the kingdom of heaven is greater than he.'
>
> (Matthew 11:2–11 NIV)

World War I Volunteers

There are few towns in Australia that don't have a memorial of some kind to the soldiers who died in the First World War. Many places have a statue of a soldier. Others have some other kind of monument. In some places the names are on a board in the town institute.

The Australian soldiers who fought in the First World War were volunteers. At the outbreak of war, men flocked to the recruiting stations to enlist. Bill Harney, the Australian author, has said: 'I was dead scared when I went to join up — scared it would be all over before I got there'.

This was a common attitude. No one wanted to miss out on the great adventure. Men lied about their age in order to be accepted, and they cried and pleaded when they were rejected for some reason or another. They all thought that they were going to go and teach the enemy a quick lesson, and soon be home again.

One wonders how many of these men would have volunteered so eagerly if they could have foreseen what the war was actually going to be like. Who could have imagined the horrors of trench warfare? Who could have imagined what an artillery bombardment would be like, with shells raining down for hours on end? Who could have imagined the shocking slaughter that would occur in places like Gallipoli and the Somme? Who could have imagined what it was like to go over the top and advance across no-man's-land in the face of a hail of machine-gun bullets, with men dropping on every side?

They were keen to go to war. They thought it was going to be a picnic. They didn't realize the terrible ordeal that lay ahead of them, and that so many were going to lose their lives.

On one occasion there were men who were keen to join Jesus, and who volunteered to be his followers. We would have expected Jesus to welcome them with open arms, but his response to them was negative.

When the first man came and said: 'I will follow you wherever you go', Jesus said to him, 'Foxes have holes, and birds have nests, but the Son of Man has nowhere to lie down and rest' (Luke 9:57,58 TEV). When Jesus invited another man to join him, the man said: 'Sir, first let me go back and bury my father', and

Jesus replied: 'Let the dead bury their own dead. You go and proclaim the Kingdom of God' (vv 59,60). The third man said: 'I will follow you, sir; but first let me go and say goodbye to my family'. Jesus said to him: 'Anyone who starts to plough and then keeps looking back is of no use to the Kingdom of God' (vv 61,62).

Jesus is not enthusiastic about these volunteers because they are too confident, too cocky about themselves. They're like the men who went off to the First World War — they don't know what they're letting themselves in for. They think that following Jesus will be easy, no big deal, and that it won't interfere with other aspects of their life.

What they don't realize is that Jesus is involved in a kind of war, that he's come to do battle with the devil, and that it will be a hard and bitter struggle. To follow Jesus will mean following him into battle, and this will involve hardship, suffering, self-denial.

Jesus wants these men to understand that following him is no picnic. This is fair dinkum. It's not something to be undertaken light-heartedly. What's required is a whole-hearted commitment based on an understanding of the consequences, a commitment that won't fail when the going gets tough.

The first volunteer says: 'I will follow you wherever you go', and Jesus replies: 'Foxes have holes, and birds have nests, but the Son of Man has nowhere to lie down and rest'. Jesus is saying to this man: 'Do you know what you're letting yourself in for? Following me will not be easy. It will not be a comfortable existence. There will be hardship and suffering. Will you still be keen to follow me when things get tough?'

A soldier caught in an artillery barrage can't go to his commanding officer and say: 'Sir, I didn't know it was going to be like this; I'd like to resign'. It's like that for us when we follow Jesus. People who are going to want to resign when the going gets tough are of no use to him. Our commitment to him needs to be whole-hearted, one that will keep going and hold firm in the face of hardship and even death.

The second man says: 'Sir, first let me go back and bury my father', and Jesus replies: 'Let the dead bury their own dead. You go and proclaim the Kingdom of God.' This man is like a soldier at the front who goes to his commanding officer and says: 'Sir, I've received a telegram saying my father's died. I'd like permission to go back home and attend the funeral.'

The soldier on active duty sometimes has to give up family commitments he would normally honour. The war takes priority.

In the same way, our relationship with Jesus takes priority over other relationships. Engaged in his service, we have to be prepared to sometimes give up things that are good in themselves and that are precious to us.

The third man says: 'I will follow you, sir; but first let me go and say goodbye to my family'. Jesus says to him; 'Anyone who starts to plough and then keeps looking back is of no use to the Kingdom of God'. This man is like a soldier about to embark for the front, who suddenly asks to be allowed to go back to his home in the country to say goodbye to his Mum.

Once you're on your way to battle, there's no turning back. Our commitment has to be a full and continuing one, even when the going gets hard and sacrifices have to be made.

This is pretty tough. Jesus seems to demand a lot from his followers. Does he ask too much? Will people really be prepared to follow him if it means hardship, sacrifice, suffering, self-denial?

People have often been prepared to make great sacrifices for something really precious to them. Many have been prepared to die for their country. People will give their lives for a belief or an ideal. Mothers will make enormous sacrifices for the sake of their children.

It's like that for us who follow Jesus. We are prepared to follow him because of what he has come to mean to us. We are prepared to commit ourselves to him because of his whole-hearted commitment of himself to us. We are prepared to make sacrifices for his sake because of the sacrifice he was prepared to make.

Just before these volunteers approached Jesus, an incident occurred which showed the way Jesus was going to follow. When the Samaritans, the traditional enemies of the Jews, refused Jesus entry to one of their villages, James and John wanted to teach them a lesson. They said to Jesus: 'Lord, do you want us to call fire down from heaven to destroy them?' (Luke 9:54). They thought that this was going to be the way of Jesus and his followers. Their attitude was like that of the soldiers who went to fight in the First World War, who thought that they were going to go and teach the enemy a quick lesson. Like those soldiers, the disciples were wrong. We are told that Jesus turned and rebuked them. This was *not* the way Jesus would follow.

Instead of teaching the enemy a quick lesson, those World War I soldiers had to face a long and terrible ordeal themselves. They had to endure great suffering. Many ended up making the supreme sacrifice.

This is the way that Jesus followed. It was the way of self-sacrifice, suffering, and death. He didn't come to call down fire from heaven on our heads. Instead, he came to give his life for us on the cross. He made the supreme sacrifice for our sake. On the cross he did battle with the devil, and defeated him. Through his death and resurrection he freed us from the devil's power, and brought us safely into God's kingdom.

Jesus made a full commitment of himself to us; that's why we can commit ourselves to him. He made the supreme sacrifice for our sake; that's why we are prepared to make sacrifices for him. We are glad to serve under him because of the great service he has rendered us.

Nowhere in the New Testament are the followers of Jesus ever spoken of as volunteers. To be a volunteer suggests a certain confidence in oneself and one's own ability. It suggests that we have something to offer Jesus.

But the fact is that we have nothing we can bring him. We are not good soldiers. Because of our sin we are really deserters, people who have run away from God. This is why we cannot be volunteers.

To become a follower of Jesus you have to be called. You can become his soldier only by being called up. It's only by God's grace that we can enter Jesus' service, and that he can begin to make good and brave soldiers of us — soldiers who will stick with him through thick and thin and not turn back when the going gets tough, soldiers who will join with him in the fight against the devil by proclaiming to people the kingdom of God.

> As the time drew near when Jesus would be taken up to heaven, he made up his mind and set out on his way to Jerusalem. He sent messengers ahead of him, who went into a village in Samaria to get everything ready for him. But the people there would not receive him, because it was clear that he was on his way to Jerusalem. When the disciples James and John saw this, they said, 'Lord, do you want us to call fire down from heaven to destroy them?'
>
> Jesus turned and rebuked them. Then Jesus and his disciples went on to another village.
>
> As they went on their way, a man said to Jesus, 'I will follow you wherever you go'.
>
> Jesus said to him, 'Foxes have holes, and birds have nests, but the Son of Man has nowhere to lie down and rest'.
>
> He said to another man, 'Follow me'.

But that man said, 'Sir, first let me go back and bury my father'.

Jesus answered, 'Let the dead bury their own dead. You go and proclaim the Kingdom of God.'

Another man said, 'I will follow you, sir; but first let me go and say goodbye to my family'.

Jesus said to him, 'Anyone who starts to plough and then keeps looking back is of no use to the Kingdom of God'.

(Luke 9:51–62 TEV)

The Australian Cuckoo

I used to think that the cuckoo was a purely European bird, but when I became interested in bird watching while living in central Australia, I discovered that there are also quite a few species of cuckoo here in Australia.

The cuckoos are an unusual group of birds, because they don't make nests of their own in which to lay their eggs and hatch out their young. Instead, the female cuckoo lays her single egg in the nest of another species of bird, and lets these other birds hatch and rear her chick. The cuckoo chicken, when it hatches, has the habit of kicking around in the nest, and usually manages to kick out the other eggs or nestlings, so it has the nest to itself.

The foster parents don't reject the cuckoo chicken, but accept it as their own and look after it and feed it until it's big enough to fend for itself. On one occasion, I observed through binoculars a young cuckoo in the nest of a pair of wrens. Wrens are very small birds, and the cuckoo chicken was at least twice as big as the adult wrens. It kept squawking in the nest with its mouth wide open, and the wrens were going flat out to and fro bringing food to feed the oversized baby.

The strange way in which the cuckoo is born and reared can be used as a picture for the mystery of Jesus' birth — a birth exactly like ours, but at the same time unique.

The cuckoo hatches from an egg and comes into the world like every other bird. In the same way, Jesus was born and came into the world exactly like every other human being.

The cuckoo chick's foster-parents recognize it as a bird just like them, and so they accept it as theirs and care for it. In the same way, Jesus is recognized as a human being exactly like us. His birth as Mary's child means that he shares our humanity in all its fullness — he is a real human being of flesh and blood.

The female cuckoo ensures that her chick will be fed and looked after by laying her egg in another bird's nest. In a similar way, God ensured that Jesus' needs as a human baby would be taken care of by providing a family and a home for him.

When Joseph found that Mary was pregnant, he was going to break his engagement with her. But God said to him: 'Don't be afraid to take Mary as your wife'. This human baby was going to need care and protection. So God provided a human family for him with Joseph and Mary, a 'nest' where he would be well looked after and brought up.

Jesus, then, was a real human being, just like you and me. But at the same time there was something different about him, he was unique.

Although the cuckoo comes into the world like any other bird, there is something unusual about its birth. It doesn't come from an egg laid by the same birds that built the nest. The egg has a different origin, it comes from outside, laid quickly in the nest by the female cuckoo while the other birds are away feeding.

In the same way, the baby Jesus, even though he is a real human baby, doesn't come into his human family in the usual way. He is not conceived and born as a result of sexual relations between Joseph and Mary. We are told that Joseph had no sexual relations with Mary before she gave birth to her son.

There is something different about the way this child was conceived and born. His mother was a virgin. He himself was conceived by the Holy Spirit. No male human being played any part in his conception. He has a unique origin — he comes from outside, from above.

Jesus is mysteriously unique. He is exactly the same as us, and yet he is also different from us. Born of Mary, he is Mary's child. But conceived by the Holy Spirit, he is also God's Son. He is completely human, but he is also God.

There is a certain mystery associated with the cuckoo. The cuckoo's egg often appears in the nests of quite small birds that build a covered nest with only a very small side entrance, too small for the adult cuckoo to get in. No one actually knows how the female cuckoo gets her egg into the nest — whether she somehow manages to lay it in the nest, or whether she lays the egg on the ground and then carries it to the nest in her beak.

There is also mystery associated with Jesus' conception and birth. None of us can understand the biology of how God could become a human embryo in Mary's womb. We cannot understand how Jesus can be both man and God at the same time.

But Jesus isn't given to us as a puzzle to unravel, as a conundrum to make us scratch our head. Instead, he's given to us as a miracle of God's grace to rejoice about.

This unique child came for a unique purpose. This purpose is made clear by the name that Joseph was told to give him. He was told to call him Jesus, the name which means *the Lord saves*, 'because he will save his people from their sins' (Matt. 1:21 TEV).

We cannot understand *how* Jesus' birth took place the way it did, but we know *why* it happened that way. It was part of God's plan to save us from our sins. God knew what he was doing. Jesus came in the way he did because it was the only way in which God could successfully carry through his plan to rescue us.

It was on the cross that Jesus carried out this unique task. He came as a human being so that he could die a human death. But he also came as God, so that his love would be strong enough to break the power of sin and death. Because he is both God and man, his victory on the cross is at the same time God's victory and our victory.

Jesus has come to us as our Immanuel, the name which means 'God is with us'. In Jesus, God has come right into the nest with us, as one of us. His presence not only gives us safety and security, but it also frees us to do things for one another that we couldn't have done otherwise. Because of this cuckoo we learn to fly.

> *This was how the birth of Jesus Christ took place. His mother Mary was engaged to Joseph, but before they were married, she found out that she was going to have a baby by the Holy Spirit. Joseph was a man who always did what was right, but he did not want to disgrace Mary publicly; so he made plans to break the engagement privately. While he was thinking about this, an angel of the Lord appeared to him in a dream and said, 'Joseph, descendant of David, do not be afraid to take Mary to be your wife. For it is by the Holy Spirit that she has conceived. She will have a son, and you will name him Jesus — because he will save his people from their sins.'*
>
> *Now all this happened in order to make what the Lord had said through the prophet come true, 'A virgin will become pregnant and have a son, and he will be called Immanuel' (which means, 'God is with us').*
>
> *So when Joseph woke up, he married Mary, as the angel of the Lord had told him to do. But he had no sexual relations with her before she gave birth to her son. And Joseph named him Jesus.*
>
> (Matthew 1:18–25 TEV)

Catherine Helen Spence and Voting Rights for Women

When the Queen visited Adelaide in March, 1986, she unveiled a statue in Light Square of a woman called Catherine Helen Spence. The plaque on the base of the statue says that she lived 1825–1910, and that she was a 'social and political reformer, writer, and preacher, who worked for children'.

One of the political reforms for which she worked hard was the right of women to vote, and South Australia became the first State in Australia, and one of the first places in the world, to give women this right.

Today we take it for granted that women should enjoy this most basic of political rights. But in many parts of the world it was something that had to be fought for over a long period of time against heavy resistance.

In South Australia women had to wait forty years after men had been given the vote before they could enjoy the same right. Many arguments were used against giving them the vote. It was claimed that it would take them away from their homes, and would create discord between husbands and wives. The country would be overrun by women orators. It was argued that women were more impulsive and excitable than men, and that it was impossible to gauge what effect the excitement of a hotly contested election would have on them — it was thought that they might collapse or become hysterical. It was feared that with the vote women would abolish war, soldiers, and 'other manly games'!

The South Australian Women's Suffrage League was formed in 1888, an organization of which Catherine Spence later became vice-president. For six years running, women's suffrage bills were before parliament. There were public debates. Catherine Spence headed a deputation to Premier Kingston. In 1894 a petition of some 11,000 signatures was presented to parliament. Finally, in December of that year, the bill received the necessary two-thirds majority in both houses.

This is an example of how a politically and socially disadvantaged group fought for a basic political right, and finally succeeded. Their only means of achieving their goal was persistent political pressure — presenting their case again and again until they were successful.

The situation was similar for a woman in a story that Jesus told. She had been wronged in some way, and was now making approaches to a judge in order to gain her legal rights against her opponent. But the judge was a corrupt man, 'who neither feared God nor respected man' (Luke 18:2 TEV), and he simply refused to act on her behalf. She was a widow, which meant that she was poor and had no money to pay him. Her opponent may have been a rich man who was bribing the judge.

But the woman wouldn't give up. She kept pestering him with her demands. She wouldn't leave him alone. And in the end he got sick of it and gave in. He said to himself: 'This woman's getting on my nerves. It looks as if the only way to get her off my back is to give her what she wants.'

Jesus held up this woman as an example for us to follow. He told the story in order to teach his disciples 'that they should always pray and never become discouraged' (Luke 18:1). He concluded his story by saying: 'Listen to what that corrupt judge said. Now, will God not judge in favour of his own people who cry to him day and night for help? Will he be slow to help them? I tell you, he will judge in their favour and do it quickly.' Then he added: 'But will the Son of Man find faith on earth when he comes?' (vv 6–8).

It would have been easy for the widow to become discouraged. For a long time she got no positive response. She could easily have given up and abandoned the struggle for her rights.

In the same way, the people fighting for the vote for women could easily have given up. In some places they had to keep up the struggle for decades against tremendous opposition. They could easily have lost heart and become discouraged.

It's easy for us to become discouraged, too. We find ourselves faced with powerful opponents in life, against whom we are helpless. We seem to have nowhere to turn for help. We call out to God, but he seems to take no notice. We pray, but get no answer. It's easy, then, to lose heart, to give up, to lose faith.

But the widow didn't give up, even when things seemed hopeless and she seemed to be getting nowhere. The fighters for women's rights kept going despite the unrelenting opposition. They kept believing that their cause was a just one, and that justice would triumph in the end. This is what kept them going, even when they could see no results for their efforts.

Statue of Catherine Helen Spence, Light Square, Adelaide, SA

Jesus tells us to be like that. He knows how strong our opponents are, and how hard it gets for us at times. But he encourages us not to give up, not to lose heart. He tells us to be persistent in calling to God for help. He tells us to keep coming to him and to keep trusting him.

Jesus asked: 'But will the Son of Man find faith on earth when he comes?' This is the important thing — to have faith in God, to keep trusting him in spite of appearances, and to keep coming to him for help.

But is such faith justified? Can God really be trusted to help? Does he really hear us when we call to him?

Jesus points out the difference between God and the judge. The judge was corrupt. He didn't care about the widow. He finally gave her justice, not because it was the right thing to do, but simply to get her off his back.

That's not what God is like. He's completely different. When we turn to him, we are not coming to someone who is unsympathetic to our needs. He understands our situation and cares about us. He hears us when we call to him for help. He is not slow in giving us a positive response.

We know that this is true, even though we can't always see it, because of Jesus and his cross. It's when we look to the cross that we see that God has already heard our cry for help and has already acted in our favour. In Jesus, he has rescued us from our cruel and ruthless opponents. Through Christ and his cross he has given us our rights — the right to call him Father, the right to belong in the security of his family, the right to successfully challenge all our opponents.

In Jesus, God has already acted in our favour. That's why we can trust him. That's why we can remain full of hope and courage in the face of whatever happens.

Don't give up. Don't lose faith in God. Keep looking to him and asking him for help. He won't let you down.

> *Then Jesus told his disciples a parable to teach them that they should always pray and never become discouraged. 'In a certain town there was a judge who neither feared God nor respected man. And there was a widow in that same town who kept coming to him and pleading for her rights, saying, "Help me against my opponent!" For a long time the judge refused to act, but at last he said to himself, "Even though I don't fear God or respect man, yet because of all the trouble this widow is giving me, I will see to it that she gets her rights. If I don't, she will keep on coming and finally wear me out!" '*
>
> *And the Lord continued, 'Listen to what that corrupt judge said. Now, will God not judge in favour of his own people who cry to him day and night for help? Will he be slow to help them? I tell you, he will judge in their favour and do it quickly. But will the Son of Man find faith on earth when he comes?*
>
> (Luke 18:1–8 TEV)

Cyclone Tracy

It was Christmas Eve, 1974, when Cyclone Tracy hit Darwin. My sister, her husband, and their two young daughters had just moved to Darwin a couple of months before. They spent that Christmas Eve huddled together under the kitchen table, with one of the walls of the house lying across the table. There, drenched and freezing cold, with the wreckage of their house flying all around them and the city being torn to bits, they found shelter and safety from that terrible storm.

The important thing in the cyclone was to find a safe place to hide, a place of protection from the storm. People found all sorts of hiding places — in bathtubs, under the bed, in the laundry, in wardrobes. The worst thing that could happen was to be caught in the open, where the air was full of flying debris, and you were exposed to the full force of the storm. It was when this happened, when they found no safe place to hide, that people got killed.

Psalm 46 speaks of a terrible catastrophe. It speaks of the earth being shaken and mountains falling into the ocean, of the seas roaring and raging, and the hills being shaken by the violence. It is speaking of a time when it seems as if the world is falling apart, as though everything is falling into chaos.

At the same time, the Psalm implies that the people of God are under attack from enemies. The powerful armies of great nations and kingdoms are moving against them and laying siege to their city.

These simple, powerful pictures refer to all the sufferings, catastrophes, troubles, threats, and dangers that confront us in life and that have the power to destroy us. There are powerful cyclonic forces out there against which we are powerless and defenceless.

There is the power of sickness, suffering, and death. There is the danger caused by our own failings and stupid mistakes. There is the terrible power of everything devilish and demonic in the world.

If we are caught out in the open, exposed to the full force of these powers, without protection, we have no hope of survival. In order to survive we need a hiding place, a place where we can find shelter and protection from the storm.

Cyclone Tracy devastation, Darwin, NT

There is such a place for us. The Psalm tells us that God is our hiding place. 'God is our shelter and strength.' 'The God of Jacob is our refuge' (vv 1,7 TEV). He is our place of shelter in the cyclone. When the storm hits and everything is falling down and flying to bits around us, we have a place of refuge with him. In the face of everything that threatens to hurt us and destroy us, he protects us and keeps us safe.

The Psalm gives expression to a fearless and unshakeable trust in God, no matter what happens. This faith is summarized in a simple but powerful way in the first line of the refrain: 'The Lord Almighty is with us' (v 7).

This was the amazing thing that the first singers of this Psalm had come to learn about God — that the Lord Almighty, the Most High God, the God who is creator and lord of the universe, had come down to them, to be close to them, to be with them. In his call of Abraham, in his promise to Jacob, in his rescue of his people from Egypt, in his revealing of his will to Moses at Mount Sinai, God had come close to his people and had graciously bound himself to them in a covenant relationship with them. In his temple in Jerusalem he was now present among them and available to them.

God has revealed himself to his people as their helper, their protector, their rescuer, their deliverer, their saviour. This is the basis for their unshakeable trust in him. He is the one who is supreme in all the world. He is the one who is powerful to defeat all evil powers and force them to surrender. He is the one who destroys the weapons of war and brings peace to his people. Because he is with them, they are safe.

Cyclone Tracy struck on Christmas Eve. It was the night on which Christians were beginning the great celebration of the birth of our Lord, of him who is called Immanuel, which means 'God is with us'. It has always seemed a terrible thing that the disaster should have occurred on that particular night, because it made it an unhappy Christmas for so many people.

But there is also a message of hope here. For thousands of people the story of that night was not just one of disaster. It was also a story of survival — of sometimes almost miraculous survival — of rescue and deliverance.

This is exactly what the story of Jesus' birth, the story of Christmas, means for us. It's a story of protection and deliverance and safety for us in the storm. It's in this child born at Bethlehem, in his life, in his death for us on the cross, and in his resurrection, that God has come close to us, to be with us. In Jesus we see that God is not a God who is against us, but the God who is for us. He does not pursue us as our judge and destroyer, but in Christ he comes to be with us as our helper and deliverer.

It's on the cross of Christ that we see 'the amazing things [God] has done on earth' (v 8). This is where we see him coming to our aid. This is where we see him triumphing over his enemies. This is where we see him doing away with strife and fighting, and bringing harmony and peace for his people.

'So we will not be afraid' (v 2). As Christians we do not have to fear being caught in the open. We do not have to fear being exposed to the full force of the cyclone, helpless before its power. We do not have to fear the terrible power of sin, death, and the devil.

In Jesus we have a hiding place, a place of refuge and safety. In Christ we have a God who is with us as our defender, our deliverer, our fortress, our shelter, our help.

This is why we can be unafraid and full of courage, no matter what happens. Psalm 46 inspired Martin Luther to write his great hymn 'A mighty fortress is our God'. With Martin Luther, and with our fellow Christians everywhere, we can confidently keep singing:

> Though devils all the world should fill,
> All eager to devour us,
> We tremble not, we fear no ill,
> They shall not overpower us.
>
> And take they our life,
> Goods, fame, child, and wife:
> Though these all be gone,
> Yet have our foes not won;
> The kingdom ours remaineth.

God is our shelter and strength,
always ready to help in times of trouble.
So we will not be afraid, even if the earth is shaken
and mountains fall into the ocean depths;
even if the seas roar and rage,
and the hills are shaken by the violence.

There is a river that brings joy to the city of God,
to the sacred house of the Most High.
God is in that city, and it will never be destroyed;
at early dawn he will come to its aid.
Nations are terrified, kingdoms are shaken;
God thunders, and the earth dissolves.

The Lord Almighty is with us;
the God of Jacob is our refuge.

Come and see what the Lord has done.
See what amazing things he has done on earth.
He stops wars all over the world;
he breaks bows, destroys spears,
and sets shields on fire.
'Stop fighting' he says, 'and know that I am God,
supreme among the nations,
supreme over the world.'

The Lord Almighty is with us;
the God of Jacob is our refuge.

(Psalm 46 TEV)

Gold Rush

With the discovery of gold in New South Wales and Victoria in the middle of the nineteenth century, a wave of gold-fever swept Australia. Lured by reports of people picking up gold nuggets from the surface of the ground, people left everything they had and flocked to the goldfields in their thousands. It was said that a third of the adult male population of Melbourne left for the diggings. Lieutenant-Governor La Trobe wrote: 'Cottages are deserted, houses to let, business is at a stand-still, and even schools are closed. In some suburbs not a man is left.'

It's hard for us today to understand the intensity of this gold-fever. But the people were mostly poor, battlers struggling to make a good life for themselves and their families. They were excited by the prospect of striking it lucky and becoming rich. There was the chance of finding that nugget that would set them up for life, and for this chance they were prepared to give up everything they had.

Jesus told a story about a man who happened to find treasure hidden in a field. He covered it up again, and was so happy that he went and sold everything he had, and then went back and bought the field.

It had been the most incredible fluke. There he was, doing some ploughing with his ox, when suddenly the plough struck something hard. He investigated, and found it was a large earthenware jar. It was full of gold coins. Someone had buried it there for safe keeping, and had never been able to come back and reclaim it.

It had taken a while to sink in that he was not just a poor labourer any more. He couldn't believe his good luck. Suddenly he had become fabulously wealthy. He could hardly restrain himself from jumping in the air, and laughing and shouting.

Jesus said: 'The Kingdom of heaven is like this' (Matt. 13:44 TEV). Being in God's kingdom, being a Christian, is like striking it lucky. It's like accidentally finding treasure, like unearthing an enormous gold nugget. It's the thrill of suddenly discovering that you are not a battler any more, but a millionaire.

How have we managed to find this great treasure? The finding of the treasure in the field was a sheer fluke. The people who found the big nuggets on the goldfields were simply lucky.

Zealous gold diggers, 1852, by S.T. Gill — La Trobe Collection, State Library of Victoria

It's like that for us. If we have found the greatest treasure of all, it's not because we were smart but because we were lucky. It's not something we can take credit for. We are like the man who finds a big nugget and can only shake his head and say: 'It was a fluke. I was lucky.'

But in the Bible it's not called luck, it's called grace. This means that if we have found this treasure, then it wasn't our doing but God's doing. It's only through God's amazing grace that you and I, who were beggars living in poverty, battlers struggling for survival, have now become millionaires.

It's God who put the nugget there for us by sending Jesus, and it's God himself who has enabled us to find this nugget by sending us the Holy Spirit. Jesus is worth his weight in gold to us because of what he did for us on the cross. We've been able to find him only because of the Holy Spirit, who has led us to him by means of God's Word.

The people who rushed to the goldfields were prepared to give up their jobs and leave everything behind for the chance of finding gold. They were like the man in Jesus' story who went and sold everything he had so that he could buy the field.

We Christians are like that, too. We are prepared to give up everything, because we know that in Jesus we've found the most valuable nugget of them all.

There will always be people, of course, quick to tell us that it's only fool's gold, and that we're mad to give up everything for something that's worthless. But we who have experienced the great thrill of finding Jesus know that this is the real thing — this is the nugget that's worth so much that there's no question about giving up everything else in order to have it.

We are the luckiest people on earth. Not only are we ourselves now set up for life, but we now also have the means to help out the other poor battlers who are still struggling to survive. With this fabulous nugget, there's enough for everyone.

The Kingdom of heaven is like this. A man happens to find a treasure hidden in a field. He covers it up again, and is so happy that he goes and sells everything he has, and then goes back and buys that field.

(Matthew 13:44 TEV)

Colonel William Light and the City of Adelaide

On Montefiore Hill in North Adelaide, with a view across Adelaide Oval and the River Torrens to the city, is Light's Vision, the statue of Colonel William Light. Light was the first Surveyor General of South Australia, and it was he who in 1836 fixed the site and laid out the city of Adelaide.

On a plaque attached to the base of the statue, there are the following extracts from Light's journal of 1839:

> *The reasons that led me to fix Adelaide where it is I do not expect to be generally understood or calmly judged of at present. My enemies, however, by disputing their validity in every particular, have done me the good service of fixing the whole of the responsibility upon me. I am perfectly willing to bear it; and I leave it to posterity, and not to them, to decide whether I am entitled to praise or to blame.*

The verdict of posterity is that Light is entitled to praise. It is generally agreed that he chose a fine site for the city, and that his plan, especially in regard to the parklands surrounding the central area, has produced an attractive city where it is pleasant to live.

John, the writer of the Book of Revelation, had an even more marvellous vision than that of Colonel Light. God gave him a vision of the city of Jerusalem, not as it exists here on earth, but a new and glorious Jerusalem, 'shining with the glory of God' (Rev. 21:11 TEV).

The city was beautifully designed and planned. It is described as 'coming down out of heaven from God' (v 10), which means that God himself is the founder of this city, and the one who has planned it and laid it out.

Who lives in this city? John's description makes it clear that the city is the place of the new people of God, the Christian church. The people of God are sometimes described as the new Israel, and John says of the city that it has a great high wall with twelve gates, and on the gates are written the names of the twelve tribes of the people of Israel. He also says that the city's wall is built on twelve foundation-stones, on which are written the names of the twelve apostles of the Lamb. This city is the home of those who belong to God and to the Lamb, Jesus Christ.

The church in John's time was only a small collection of scattered congregations. In addition, many of the Christians were being persecuted because of their faith in Christ. There was nothing impressive about the church at that time. It was a hard-pressed and threatened minority.

But the vision of the church that John gives these suffering, persecuted Christians is of something wonderful, magnificent, extraordinarily beautiful, unimaginably glorious. 'The city shone like a precious stone, like a jasper, clear as crystal' (v 11).

John reminds us that the church of God, always despised, mocked, and attacked, is in reality something glorious, and that it's a wonderful thing to be a resident of this city.

In describing the beauty of the new Jerusalem, John mentions two remarkable things about it — it has no temple, and neither the sun nor the moon shine there.

Adelaide has been called the city of churches, and one of its landmarks, prominently visible from Light's Vision, is St Peter's Cathedral at the northern end of Adelaide Oval.

But God's city, the new Jerusalem, has no temple. We would expect a city designed by God to be dominated by a magnificent cathedral, just as the earthly Jerusalem was dominated by the temple. The temple was the focal-point of the city, its great landmark, its main attraction.

But in the new Jerusalem there is no cathedral, no temple. Its place is taken by God himself and by the Lamb, Jesus. 'I did not see a temple in the city, because its temple is the Lord God Almighty and the Lamb' (v 22).

The city of God does not have its focal-point, its centre, in a particular place or building, but in a person: Jesus. Jesus is our temple, because it's in him that God meets us and we meet God. God and Jesus are the focal-point, the landmark for this city. They themselves are its great feature, the great attraction for people coming to live here.

The other thing about the city is that it 'has no need of the sun or the moon to shine on it' (v 23). No sun! What a disaster for us sun-loving, sun-worshipping Australians! It looks like the end of our outdoor sporting and leisure activities, our sunbaking and surf, our barbecues and beer.

Not at all. The sun is gone, but in its place is something better: God and the Lamb. 'The glory of God shines on [the city], and the Lamb is its lamp' (v 23). The Lamb, Jesus, takes the place of the sun. In this city we can sunbake continually in the sun that is

Jesus. We can soak in the warmth from his rays, and be constantly renewed and invigorated by his energy.

Adelaide is Light's city. The new Jerusalem is the city of light, because Jesus is its light — the source of everything healthy, healing, and good.

It's not an easy thing to found a city. It happens only through the sacrifice of time and effort. Colonel Light worked under very difficult conditions and often against strong and bitter opposition, which probably hastened his early death.

The founding of God's city was also a long and difficult process against bitter opposition. It was carried through only because of the Lamb's willingness to sacrifice himself by dying on the cross. The glorious city that exists for our benefit today is the result of his blood, sweat, and tears.

Make your home in this city, with God and the Lamb. It's the best place there is to live.

> The Spirit took control of me, and the angel carried me to the top of a very high mountain. He showed me Jerusalem, the Holy City, coming down out of heaven from God and shining with the glory of God. The city shone like a precious stone, like a jasper, clear as crystal. It had a great, high wall with twelve gates and with twelve angels in charge of the gates. On the gates were written the names of the twelve tribes of the people of Israel. There were three gates on each side: three on the east, three on the south, three on the north, and three on the west. The city's wall was built on twelve foundation-stones, on which were written the names of the twelve apostles of the Lamb...
>
> I did not see a temple in the city, because its temple is the Lord God Almighty and the Lamb. The city has no need of the sun or the moon to shine on it, because the glory of God shines on it, and the Lamb is its lamp.
>
> (Revelation 21:10–14,22,23 TEV)

Winning the Premiership

In 1986 my son and I went to watch our church football team play in the grand final. A member of our congregation was playing at full-forward, and he'd invited us to come and barrack for them.

It was an exciting match. Our team went into the game as underdogs, but they ended up winning convincingly, and so won the premiership.

There were scenes of great jubilation in the dressing-rooms afterwards. All the players and supporters were ecstatic. They kept hugging each other and saying: 'We did it! We did it!'

And they sang. The club song was sung as a victory song, again and again, at full strength, as loudly as possible. Blokes who at other times would have protested that they couldn't sing a note were singing at the tops of their voices. They were singing because they'd gone top, they'd won the premiership.

On the shore of the Red Sea the people of Israel sang, too. They had been rank underdogs, but had just won a great victory. They had been in a completely hopeless situation, trapped between the horses and chariots of the Egyptian army on the one side and the Red Sea on the other. There had seemed no hope of winning. They would either be massacred or taken back into slavery in Egypt.

But now they saw the Egyptian soldiers lying dead on the seashore. God had opened a way for them through the water, and when the soldiers followed, the waters returned and covered them. The enemy army had been destroyed. They themselves had been rescued. They were safe. They were free.

And so they sang. But the songs they sang were not songs in praise of themselves — their own soldiers, their own exploits in battle, their own courage and strength and skill. Instead, they were songs in praise of the Lord. As Miriam and the other women danced and played their tambourines, the Israelites sang: 'I will sing to the Lord, because he has won a glorious victory; he has thrown the horses and their riders into the sea' (Exod. 15:1 TEV).

This great victory was completely God's doing. The people had contributed nothing toward it at all. That's why their songs praised God as the mighty warrior, their defender, their rescuer, their saviour. 'The Lord is my strong defender; he is the one who has saved me.' 'The Lord is a warrior; the Lord is his name.' 'Your right hand, Lord, is awesome in power; it breaks the enemy in pieces' (vv 2,3,6).

God had come to the help of his people when they were threatened and in danger. That's why they danced and celebrated and sang their victory songs.

Their situation had completely changed. They had been on the brink of defeat, but had ended up winning. They had been staring death in the face, but had escaped with their lives. They had been slaves, but now they were free. Their situation had been hopeless, but now they had a future to look forward to.

When a football team wins a premiership, it's an event which club members and supporters never forget. Premiership pennants, trophies, and photos are displayed in the clubrooms, and whenever a club dinner is held the premiership victories of the past are remembered and celebrated.

It was the same with the people of Israel — they never forgot the great victory at the Red Sea. Hundreds of years after the event, they kept on remembering it and celebrating it in the annual Passover Festival.

And whenever they did this, whenever they sat down to eat the Passover meal in their homes, they sang again their victory songs. One of these songs was Psalm 114, a song which celebrates the rescue from Egypt including the victory at the Red Sea. Other songs sung at the Passover meal were Psalms 115–118, songs which praise God for rescue from death and for victory over enemies.

It was these victory songs which Jesus and his disciples also sang when they celebrated the Passover together on the night before Jesus was put to death on the cross. We are told that at the end of the meal 'they sang a hymn and went out to the Mount of Olives' (Matt. 26:30 TEV).

It was appropriate that they sang these songs that night, not only because they were remembering and celebrating the great win at the Red Sea, but also because God was about to win another great victory, the greatest of them all.

Jesus' death on the cross, and his resurrection, are the great victory that God has won for us and that we Christians celebrate. This victory is like the one he won for the people of Israel at the Red Sea, but it goes far beyond it. On the cross, Jesus set us free from slavery to sin and death. Here he destroyed the power of our great enemy, the devil. Through his death, he has brought us safe and sound into God's kingdom, and has given us eternal life with God.

None of this was our doing. It was achieved completely by God. Our situation was completely hopeless — we were under sin's power and faced certain death. But against all expectation, God was good to us and rescued us. On the cross he won a great victory for us.

This is why Christians have always sung, why the Christian church has always been a singing church. We sing because we have something to sing about — like a football team that's won a premiership, like the Israelites at the Red Sea. We are always singing because every Sunday is a celebration of that great Sunday on which Jesus rose from the dead. Every Holy Communion is a victory dinner commemorating his great win over sin and death.

Anyone who plays sport has to be prepared to lose. There is often the disappointment of not succeeding, of just failing to win. I once played in a football grand final which we lost by two points on the last kick of the day.

In our life, too, we experience the disappointment of failure and loss. Our fondest hopes and best intentions are often defeated.

But in the face of every failure and loss we can keep singing our victory songs. We can do this because Jesus, through his death and resurrection, has won a great premiership victory for us, and no one can ever take that victory away from us.

> Then Moses and the Israelites sang
> this song to the Lord:
> 'I will sing to the Lord, because he has won a glorious
> victory;
> he has thrown the horses and their riders into the sea.
> The Lord is my strong defender;
> he is the one who has saved me.
> He is my God, and I will praise him,
> my father's God, and I will sing about his greatness.
> The Lord is a warrior;
> the Lord is his name.

> 'He threw Egypt's army and its chariots into the sea;
> the best of its officers were drowned in the Red Sea.
> The deep sea covered them;
> they sank to the bottom like a stone.

'Your right hand, Lord, is awesome in power;
  it breaks the enemy in pieces.
In majestic triumph you overthrow your foes;
  your anger blazes out and burns them up like straw.
You blew on the sea and the water piled up high;
  it stood up straight like a wall;
  the deepest part of the sea became solid.
The enemy said, "I will pursue them and catch them;
  I will divide their wealth and take all I want;
  I will draw my sword and take all they have."
But one breath from you, Lord, and the Egyptians were
    drowned;
  they sank like lead in the terrible water.

'Lord, who among the gods is like you?
  Who is like you, wonderful in holiness?
  Who can work miracles and mighty acts like yours?'
                                    (Exodus 15:1–11 TEV)

Survival in the Outback

'Tourist Dies in Outback Ordeal' was the front-page headline of the Adelaide *Advertiser* on January 8, 1988. The 46-year-old man had died of thirst after spending five days in above 40°C heat in South Australia's far north. He had walked about 30 km trying to get help for his wife and son after the family's station wagon became bogged in a creek near Lake Cadibarrawirracanna, between Coober Pedy and William Creek. His wife and son, who had remained with the vehicle, were eventually found safe and sound.

Outback travel, particularly in the middle of summer, can be dangerous. When vehicles break down on lonely bush tracks, or become bogged in sandy creek crossings, people can perish in that harsh environment.

One of the rules for outback travel is to stay with your vehicle if you get into trouble. In normal circumstances it mightn't be hard for a fit person to walk 30, 40, or even 50 km to get help. But it's a different matter trying to do it in the middle of an outback summer, with the temperature way over 40°C. In those conditions, a person quickly becomes dehydrated and can soon die.

In addition, it's hard for searchers to spot an isolated individual from the air in the vast expanses of the outback. A vehicle can be spotted much more easily.

The only chance of survival, when you're in trouble in the outback, is for someone to find you. You just have to sit tight and wait for this to happen. In the meantime, the important thing is to conserve energy and avoid dehydration. The best thing is to find a shady spot, keep still, and do absolutely nothing.

Jesus and his disciples came to the village where the sisters Mary and Martha lived, and were welcomed into their home. Martha was a kind and good person, who wanted to do the right thing for Jesus. She ended up having to do all the work on her own, because Mary simply sat there enjoying Jesus' company.

Eventually it became too much for Martha, and she came to Jesus and said: 'Lord, don't you care that my sister has left me to do all the work by myself? Tell her to come and help me!' (Luke 10:40 TEV).

On an outback road

It seemed a reasonable request. Jesus would surely agree, and Mary could hardly refuse when he told her to go and help her sister.

But to everyone's surprise, Jesus stuck up for Mary and defended what she was doing. At the same time, he understood how Martha was feeling and was very gentle with her. 'Martha, Martha!' he said. 'You are worried and troubled over so many things, but just one is needed. Mary has chosen the right thing, and it will not be taken away from her' (vv 41,42).

Jesus used this simple domestic situation to teach a lesson. There is a time, he says, when the right thing, the one thing that's needed, is to stay where you are and do nothing. There's a time when it's important simply to keep still.

When is it important to do this? When Jesus is there. It's in the presence of Jesus that we need to keep still.

In the outback the time for doing nothing is when you're in trouble and have no hope of getting out of it by yourself. Your only hope then is for someone to come and find you. Until that happens, the best thing is simply to sit tight and wait. If you try to do something yourself, it only makes the situation worse — it actually lessens your chances of survival.

It's important for us to be still and do nothing in the presence of Jesus, because he's the only one who can rescue us. We're in big trouble. Because of our sin, we are hopelessly bogged out here in the desert, with nothing we can do to help ourselves. We are in danger of perishing.

Our only hope of rescue lies with Jesus. There's nothing we can do ourselves. Everything depends on him. He's the only one who can set us free from our sins. He's the only one who can save us from death. He's the only one who can find us and bring us safely back to God.

That's why we have to keep still. We have to do nothing, so that he can do everything needed to save us.

There is a time for being busy. There is a time for being active in the service of our Lord, for working hard in helping and caring for one another.

But first we have to learn to be passive, to keep still in the presence of Jesus. Our natural inclination is to refuse help, to want to do something for ourselves. We like to think we can solve our own problems. But we have to keep learning that in the face of sin and death we can do nothing to save ourselves. Everything depends on God and his grace.

'Just one thing is needed', Jesus told Martha. The one thing that is absolutely essential, the one thing we need above everything else, is Jesus himself. He's the only one who can rescue us from the trouble we're in.

We need to keep still so that he can find us and rescue us. It's important that we do nothing, so that he can do everything for us.

> *As Jesus and his disciples went on their way, he came to a village where a woman named Martha welcomed him in her home. She had a sister named Mary, who sat down at the feet of the Lord and listened to his teaching.*
>
> *Martha was upset over all the work she had to do, so she came and said, 'Lord, don't you care that my sister has left me to do all the work by myself? Tell her to come and help me!'*
>
> *The Lord answered her, 'Martha, Martha! You are worried and troubled over so many things, but just one is needed. Mary has chosen the right thing, and it will not be taken away from her.'*
>
> (Luke 10:38–42 TEV)

The Convict and the Parson

In New South Wales, in the early days of the colony as a convict settlement, convicts who committed an offence were given punishments that today seem appallingly brutal.

The punishment which was used most frequently, and which was most feared by the convicts, was being 'married to the three sisters' — being tied to the triangle and flogged. One historian has written: 'Language can give only a pale imitation of the grisly reality of blood-soaked flesh being methodically stripped from a man's back by the flail of the professional scourger'. There are accounts of the surgeons required to attend each flogging turning away sickened by the sight of the deliberate damage to human tissue which they would have to try to repair.

It was customary to give 25 lashes for a slight offence, and 50 lashes for a more serious offence. Usually a whip of knotted cords was used which caused blood to flow at the first stroke.

One man who witnessed a flogging described the pair of scourgers who took turn about on the victim as being 'bespattered with blood like a couple of butchers'. He watched one of their victims walk across the yard 'with blood that had run from his lacerated flesh squashing out of his shoes at every step he took'. A dog was licking the blood off the triangle, and ants were carrying away 'great pieces of human flesh' that the lash had scattered about the ground.

The men who carried out these floggings were former convicts, men with the required strength and sadism, who were given training on dummies in Hyde Park. When it became hard to find enough floggers for all the police posts throughout New South Wales, men were encouraged to volunteer for the job by the offer of eight pence a day above constable's wages, plus unlimited rations.

Among the convicts, the floggers were the most hated and despised of men. There are accounts of men, after they had been flogged, deliberately spitting in the flogger's face. One man told Black Francis (scourger at Goulburn, later murdered by one of his victims) that 'he couldn't flog hard enough to kill a butterfly'.

The floggers were hated so bitterly because they were men who had allied themselves with the hated authorities against their fellow-convicts for personal gain.

The Reverend Samuel Marsden was one of the first clergymen to serve in New South Wales. He was a respectable and morally upright man, whose achievements were considerable. Apart from performing his regular pastoral duties, he established a Sunday-school, promoted the building of a new church, and assisted in the establishing of a home and a school for orphans.

He came to despair of the possibility of reclaiming the souls of convicts and Aborigines; they were so steeped in vice and idleness, and defeated the best of regulations with their 'invincible depravity'.

He turned his attention to New Zealand, and was the first to send missionary expeditions and establish white settlements there. He made important contributions to the development of agriculture in New South Wales, and was prominent in the public affairs of the colony.

But there was another side to this man, too. In 1795 he was appointed magistrate and superintendent of government affairs at Parramatta where he lived. As a magistrate, he became known for his extreme severity. He came to be called 'the flogging parson'. He saw Parramatta as such a sink of iniquity that morality could be preserved only by the most rigorous disciplinary means. On one occasion, quite illegally, he and another judge had a convict flogged mercilessly in an attempt to get information from him about suspected hidden weapons.

In addition, Marsden was a man who refused to associate with ex-convicts on equal terms. He regarded the 'convict stain' as something that a person could never get rid of. On one occasion, Governor Macquarie appointed him to serve on a committee with two ex-convicts who had become wealthy and respected men. He refused to accept the position. He considered that associating in this way with these men would damage the reputation of his sacred office.

Jesus once told a parable for the benefit of 'people who were sure of their own goodness and despised everybody else' (Luke 18:9 TEV). The story was about two men who went to the temple in Jerusalem to pray. One of them was a tax collector, and the other was a Pharisee.

The tax collector was a person who was despised and hated by his fellow Jews, just as the flogger was despised and hated by his fellow convicts. This was because the tax collector, like the flogger, was someone who had allied himself with the hated authorities (the Romans) against his own people for personal gain. He was able to use his position to rip people off and line his own pockets.

The tax collector was the lowest of the low. He was a collaborator and a crook. His fellow Jews regarded him with the same loathing with which the convicts regarded the flogger. He was the most despicable and contemptible of people. He was a social and religious outcast.

The Pharisee was like the Reverend Samuel Marsden. He was the respectable and morally upright person of Jesus' day, who performed his religious duties to the letter. He had a clean moral record. He could present an impressive list of his achievements and his contributions to society.

But he was also self-righteous, and hard and intolerant in his attitude to others. He was careful not to damage his reputation by mixing with riff-raff. Just as Samuel Marsden would never mix with people bearing the 'convict stain', so the Pharisee would never have anything to do with people like tax collectors.

In the temple these two men prayed.

> The Pharisee stood apart by himself and prayed, 'I thank you, God, that I am not greedy, dishonest, or an adulterer, like everybody else. I thank you that I am not like that tax collector over there. I fast two days a week, and I give you a tenth of my income.'
> But the tax collector stood at a distance and would not even raise his face to heaven, but beat on his breast and said, 'God, have pity on me, a sinner!' 'I tell you', said Jesus, 'the tax collector, and not the Pharisee, was in the right with God when he went home. For everyone who makes himself great will be humbled and everyone who humbles himself will be made great.'
>
> (Luke 18:11–14 TEV)

What's astonishing here is that it's not the Pharisee, not the respectable and morally upright parson, but the tax collector, the despicable and contemptible flogger, whose prayer is heard and who is accepted by God.

God is not the friend of the proud and self-righteous person, but of the person who's prepared to admit that he's been wrong. He is not the friend of the person who is sure of his own goodness, but of the person who knows and acknowledges that he has not done the right thing. He is not the friend of the hard-hearted moralist, but of the broken-hearted sinner.

None of us can brag in the presence of God. It's no good holding up our good deeds to him. He sees past our respectable exterior. He sees that the morally upright Reverend Samuel Marsden is also a cruel man lacking in compassion, just as much a sinner as the offending convict he sentences to be flogged. We are all equally guilty in God's eyes, all of us no better than the convict, the tax collector, the criminal, and all equally deserving of punishment.

But in spite of this, God didn't take a hard attitude towards us. He didn't despair of the possibility of reclaiming us. He didn't treat us with contempt and keep his distance from us.

Instead, he had pity on us. In Jesus he came close to us and befriended us. He mixed with the tax collectors, with the social and religious outcasts. He understood us and accepted us. He identified with us.

He identified so closely with us convicts that he suffered our fate, our punishment. For our sake he went to the triangle and had the flesh systematically stripped from his back by the Roman floggers. Then he was taken out to be executed on the scaffold as a criminal between two convicts.

Jesus became a convict, and died a convict's death, so that we convicts could go free. He suffered a convict's flogging so that we could escape punishment. By his death and resurrection he erased the convict stain of our sin and made us right with God.

God never refuses us when we come to him as sinners who are prepared to own up to the fact. In Jesus he has been good to us beyond anything we deserved. We are sinners living under God's pardon.

God's acceptance of us in Christ frees us from our self-righteousness and hard-heartedness. It has power to change us, to set us free from our guilty past, to give us new life with God and a new future. It frees us to begin showing to one another the compassion, the understanding, and the acceptance that God has shown us in Jesus.

Killing the Snake

I'll always remember the first time I killed a snake. It happened while we were living at Hermannsburg in central Australia. It was a big snake, a King Brown, about a metre and a quarter long.

We had a big yard around our house, and my wife Diana had caught sight of the snake in a section of the yard that had become overgrown with thick grass after rain. I decided that I would have to get rid of the grass to see if the snake was still there, and if it was, I'd have to kill it.

So I spent that afternoon working with spade and hoe to clean up the yard. I got a fright when I disturbed the snake and saw it go down into a shallow hole that had been dug to get at a water pipe. It disappeared there under dry leaves and bark from the big gum trees in our yard. At least I now knew where it was.

All the time I was working, I kept close to me a doubled-over length of steel fencing wire about a metre and a half in length. I had been assured many times by various people that a length of wire was the best thing for killing a snake, so I'd decided that this was the weapon I'd use.

I was pretty scared because I'd never tackled a snake before, and I kept picking up my length of wire to get the feel of it. It was hard to believe that it would actually work. It didn't feel heavy enough or strong enough. It felt too skinny, too pliable, too flimsy.

Finally I'd cleared away all the grass. I was standing there wondering how I was going to get the snake out, when suddenly its head appeared from under the debris. By the time I'd turned and grabbed my wire off the ground, it was out of the hole and already had its head through a gap in the iron fence.

I came down with the wire as hard as I could, and in an instant the snake's back was broken and it was immobilized. Still shaky with fright, I was able to finish it off quickly.

As a result of that one hit, I will now tell anyone that a piece of fencing wire is the best weapon for killing a snake. It felt weak and flimsy, but the whip in that steel made it come down with tremendous force, easily strong enough to break a snake's back. Because it could bend, it flattened itself along the uneven ground, making it virtually impossible for me to miss. And unlike something rigid like a stick, there was no danger of it breaking.

The weapon that had seemed so flimsy turned out to be deadly.

Out in the desert, south of the Dead Sea, God gave the people of Israel a weapon against snakes. He himself had sent the poisonous snakes as a punishment for the people. They had lost their patience, and had spoken against God and Moses. They complained: 'Why did you bring us out of Egypt to die in this desert, where there is no food or water? We can't stand any more of this miserable food' (Num. 21:5 TEV). Then God sent the snakes, and many of the people were bitten and died.

The people realized what they had done. They had forgotten the good things God had done for them in rescuing them from slavery in Egypt, and in uniting himself with them in a covenant at Mount Sinai. They had forgotten his promise that he would care for them and protect them, and that he would give their descendants the land he was leading them to.

'The people came to Moses and said, "We sinned when we spoke against the Lord and against you. Now pray to the Lord to take these snakes away." So Moses prayed for the people' (v 7).

God heard the prayer and answered it. He took pity on his people, and came to their help. But not by getting rid of the snakes. He told Moses to make a snake out of bronze and put it on a pole, and he promised that anyone who was bitten and who looked at it would be healed.

Many of the people must have shaken their heads when they heard what was being done. A metal snake on a pole? What sort of weapon was that against poisonous snakes? They would have had more doubts about this than I did about my length of wire. Many must have said: 'It'll never work'.

But it did work. Those who were bitten and who looked at the bronze snake didn't die. They recovered. How did it happen? How could a metal snake on a pole save people from snake-bite? It was only because God and his promise were connected with it. God was teaching his people to look away from themselves and their own problems and sufferings, and to look to him. He wanted to teach them that no matter what painful and deadly things were staring them in the face, they could trust him and his goodness, they could rely on his promise.

God has provided for us a weapon against snakes, against everything that can sting and hurt and poison and kill. Not a snake on a pole, but a man on a cross.

Black snake

*As Moses lifted up the bronze snake on a pole in the
desert, in the same way the Son of Man must be lifted up, so
that everyone who believes in him may have eternal life
(John 3:14,15 TEV).*

If we had been told that this was going to be God's weapon
against the devil and his poison, we would have shaken our heads
in disbelief. A man dying on a cross? What good will that do? It'll
never work.

But it did work. Just as the length of wire was the perfect
weapon against the snake, so Jesus is God's perfect weapon
against the devil. Just like that wire, Jesus looked weak and flimsy.
It looked as if they could bend him any way they liked. But there
was a strength and whip in this steel wire, and on the cross, with
one hit, he broke the devil's back.

Of all the thousands of people who have been crucified, only this one man, Jesus, has the power to save us from dying. This is because God himself is in Jesus, and his powerful Word of promise is connected with his cross. God's love, strong as steel, is hidden in Jesus and his cross. This is what breaks the devil's back for us and saves our life.

When the snakes are attacking you, when you are the target of the devil's venom, look to Christ and his cross. Take hold of the piece of wire that God has provided for you there. Trust God's promise. Trust that length of wire, even though it looks weak, as if it wouldn't work. Jesus is the perfect weapon against the devil, against all the snakes that can sting and kill. He has broken the devil's back. Trust him, and you will live.

> The Israelites left Mount Hor by the road that leads to the Gulf of Aqaba, in order to go round the territory of Edom. But on the way the people lost their patience and spoke against God and Moses. They complained, 'Why did you bring us out of Egypt to die in this desert, where there is no food or water? We can't stand any more of this miserable food!' Then the Lord sent poisonous snakes among the people, and many Israelites were bitten and died. The people came to Moses and said, 'We sinned when we spoke against the Lord and against you. Now pray to the Lord to take these snakes away.' So Moses prayed for the people. Then the Lord told Moses to make a metal snake and put it on a pole, so that anyone who was bitten could look at it and be healed. So Moses made a bronze snake and put it on a pole. Anyone who had been bitten would look at the bronze snake and be healed.
>
> (Numbers 21:4–9 TEV)

The Hurricane Lamp in the Storm

*Your word is a lamp to guide me
and a light for my path.*
(Psalm 119:105 TEV)

Ivan Southall's novel *Over the Top* tells the story of Perry Benson, an eleven-year-old boy who's woken up by his father on a stormy night at 2.00 am. His mother is about to have a baby, and they have to get her to the hospital. They live on an isolated property without electricity and without a telephone.

Perry and his mother wait in the darkness at the back door while Mr Benson goes down the path to get the car out of the shed and switch on the car lights. They wait for a long time, but nothing happens. They call out, but get no answer. Finally they go out into the rain to investigate. They find him lying on the path unconscious. In the dark he has tripped over Perry's billycart and hit his head on the rocks at the edge of the garden bed.

It's left mainly to Perry to drag his father inch by inch along the path to the shed, and then manhandle him into the back seat of the little Morris with the canvas hood. Then Perry's mother, who hasn't driven for years, tries to back out of the shed, but the car gets away from her and runs off the drive down the slope, where it gets hopelessly bogged.

Mrs Benson now decides that the only thing is for Perry to walk to Mr Morgan's, their nearest neighbour, who has a phone. She explains that it's too dangerous to go herself — she could slip or fall in the dark, and the baby could get hurt.

Perry isn't keen to go, not only because it's cold and stormy and dark, but also because he's frightened of Mr Morgan. His property has barbed-wire fences, locked gates, and signs saying 'Traps set. Baits laid.' Perry's father and Mr Morgan have always been enemies because of their different political views.

But Perry has to go; there's no other way to get help. His mother tells him that he'll be all right if he takes the hurricane lamp. So he goes into the shed out of the wind, gets the lamp lit, and sets off for Mr Morgan's.

It's a scary journey for a young boy, even though it's not really very far, and he worries about the lamp going out.

Half a mile to Mr Morgan's. Up the hill and over the top and down the other side. Half a mile when the sun was lighting up the day, but more like miles now. Everything wet and black. Everything roaring with wind. Miles and miles. Little yellow lamp flickering and flaring, blowing out soot. Sooting up the glass. Glass spattering and hissing with rain splashing on it. Great big dollops of rain falling from the trees. Trees like giants as tall as night standing in rows, leg to leg, side by side, bombarding him with dollops of rain as big as stones. Giants sometimes stepping back a stride, or slipping closer, as he floundered by, Perry catching them from the corner of his eye.

Don't you touch me, trees. You stay there. You're not supposed to move around. You're not allowed.

Over the top and down the other side where shapeless creatures that should have lived in dreams were out hunting for boys who should have been in bed. Creatures with too many heads and too many feet and horrible wailing cries. Two a.m. creatures.

I'm hurrying, Mum, like you said.

Not because I'm scared.

Lamp jigging up and down. Don't you go out, lamp. If you go out I think I'll die.

The lamp doesn't go out, and he manages not to drop it while climbing over the locked gate. He gets to Mr Morgan's house. There's more drama along the way, but Mr Morgan comes to the help of his neighbour, and the baby is eventually born safely, even if Mr Benson has to deliver it himself.

Perry probably could not have made that journey through the storm without the hurricane lamp. Without it, he could have lost his way or suffered serious injury like his father. The lamp enabled him to make the dangerous and scary journey safely.

Other lives were depending on that lamp too. His father was injured, and needed medical attention. If anything were to go wrong with the birth, the lives of his mother and the baby could be in danger too. To Perry and his family that night, the hurricane lamp was a real lifesaver.

'Your word is a lamp to guide me and a light for my path.' In the middle of the storm, in the middle of the night when it's pitch black, God provides a hurricane lamp for us — his Word. With this lamp we can find our way safely through the darkness without getting hurt. This lamp saves our life.

God's Word is a lifesaving word because it brings us Jesus. Mr Morgan came out on a stormy night to help the neighbour who had always hated him and been his enemy. In Jesus and his cross we see the God who came out into the darkness and the storm to help us who were his enemies.

God's Word is the hurricane lamp that guides us to Jesus, who saves our life. Through his death and resurrection he has overcome the darkness of our sin and has destroyed the dark powers of death and the devil. Through him God has brought us out of darkness into his marvellous light.

Perry said: 'Don't you go out, lamp. If you go out I think I'll die.' He knew that if the lamp went out or he dropped it he was in big trouble.

We would be in big trouble too if the lamp of God's Word were ever to go out on us. Without this Word we will die. It's only with God's Word that we can find Jesus, the only one who can save our life.

The world can be a dangerous and scary place. There are times when our life is threatened, when we must go through darkness and storm. But in his Word God has provided us with a good hurricane lamp to take with us.

Hang on to this lamp — your life depends on it. Don't drop it. Hold it tight and carry it with you always. With this lamp you can walk through the blackest night and the wildest storm, and find your way safely.

Charles Kingsford Smith and the 'Southern Cross'

On May 31, 1928, a three-engined Fokker monoplane took off from San Francisco to attempt the first crossing of the Pacific Ocean by air. The pilot was Charles Kingsford Smith (Smithy, as he was known to Australians), one of the world's greatest aviators. His co-pilot, Charles Ulm, was also an Australian. With them were two Americans — Harry Lyon (navigator) and James Warner (radio operator). The Australians had named their aeroplane the *Southern Cross*.

Ten days later, after touching down in Hawaii, Fiji, and Brisbane, they landed at Mascot Airport in Sydney, to be welcomed by an estimated crowd of 300,000 people.

This outstanding achievement is all the more remarkable in view of the difficulties involved in air navigation at that time — radar was unheard of, radio navigation was in a rudimentary stage, and few air navigational instruments existed. Most of the navigating on this trip was done by what was called 'dead reckoning', a combination of chart, compass, clock, and sheer guesswork. Harry Lyon, the navigator, had an ordinary ship's sextant for taking sightings of the stars, but it wasn't often that the aeroplane, heavily loaded with fuel, could get above the clouds.

The problems were made worse by the fact that, of the 83½ hours spent in the air, nearly half that time was spent battling violent storms. During the night on the longest stage between Hawaii and Fiji, conditions were so bad that Smithy decided to sacrifice precious fuel to seek better conditions at higher altitude.

With the driving rain coming straight into the open cockpit, they slowly climbed through the inky blackness, Smithy flying in circles to gain height while avoiding the worst of the storm. Suddenly they burst through the clouds, and were excited to see glittering above them in the clear sky the Southern Cross. Not only did they now have a chance to check their bearings, but the sight of the constellation after which their aeroplane was named lifted their spirits enormously.

The wise men who came from the east looking for the baby Jesus were attempting a journey that no one had ever made before. They were the first Gentiles, the first non-Jews, to

Replica of the 'Southern Cross'

attempt to find the Messiah, the new-born king of the Jews. It was a long and difficult journey that they undertook, and dangerous.

They navigated by means of a star, a special star that had appeared in the sky. They came first of all to Jerusalem and consulted with King Herod. He directed them, on the basis of Old Testament prophecies, to the town of Bethlehem.

As they left Jerusalem and looked up into the night sky, they saw again the same star they had seen in the east. The sight of this star lifted their spirits enormously. 'When they saw it, how happy they were, what joy was theirs!' (Matt. 2:10 TEV).

With the help of the star, they were able to find what they were looking for. In a house in Bethlehem they found Mary and Joseph and the baby Jesus. Their journey was at an end. They had found their king, their saviour. They knelt down and worshipped him, and gave him their precious gifts.

This child born at Bethlehem is the goal of our life, too. It is crucial for us, too, that we find him.

The wise men set out to find him because they somehow knew that their future, their destiny, their whole life, depended on this child. What they were doing must have seemed crazy to others (just as Smithy's attempt on the Pacific seemed crazy to many), but for them it was something they simply had to do. It was so important that they were prepared to undergo a long and arduous journey to reach their goal. They somehow knew that of all the millions of people in the world this one child was the one on whom their life depended, the one they had to find.

It was like the second leg of Smithy's flight, the one between Hawaii and Fiji. After 34½ hours in the air, and after battling storms and flying in circles during the night, in all that vast expanse of ocean they had to be able to locate that one speck of land. Even a small error of navigation would mean missing their mark, in which case they would soon run out of fuel and perish in the ocean.

It's like that for us. In all the vast ocean of humanity, it is absolutely crucial that we find that one person, Mary's baby born at Bethlehem. It's a matter of life and death. If we find him we will have a safe landing place and we will be all right. If we fail to find him, if we go off course, we will perish.

How can we be sure of finding him? How can we navigate correctly and avoid going off course? How can we be sure of not ending up in the ocean?

The wise men had a star to guide them. Smithy and his companions used the stars to find their way. Is there a star for us by which we can find our way?

As a child living in the country, I remember being told how to use the Southern Cross to find my way at night if I was lost. You follow a line from the top of the cross along its main axis for a distance of about three lengths of the cross, and that gives you south. So if you can locate the Southern Cross, you can always know in what direction you're going. Many people have used the Southern Cross in this way to help them find their way.

We have a star to guide us, by which we can find our way, and this star is the cross of Jesus. If we are to find our King, if we are to find our Saviour, then we must look to the cross. It seems an unlikely place to look for a king — a man hanging on a cross, but it's the only place we'll ever find him. Only the cross can guide us to that one speck of land in the whole vast ocean of humanity where there is a safe landing-place for us.

If we can locate the cross of Christ, that's when we will experience the same joy that the wise men had when they saw the star, the same thrill that Smithy and his companions felt when they caught sight of the Southern Cross. We will experience this great joy because there on the cross we will find the one who has conquered for us the vast distance between us and God, the one who has battled the storms for us and who brings us safely through, the one who carries us to a safe landing place with God.

It's at the cross that we find our journey is at an end, the goal has been reached. All our striving and searching are finished; because in the one who was born at Bethlehem and who died on the cross for me, all my deepest longings are met, all my hopes are finally fulfilled.

When I was living in central Australia I got interested in the stars because of the clear night skies, and for many years I looked for someone who could explain the stars to me — their movements and their names.

There are many of our fellow Australians — neighbours, friends, family, acquaintances — who are in a similar situation. They are waiting for someone to show them the cross and how to use it to find their way. We who know how to locate the cross and how to use it to find our way have an obligation to pass this information on to others. They need this just as much as we do, so that they can find the right direction for their life, and can find their way to Jesus and the joy and safety that he gives.

When you look up at the stars, remember the star that guided the wise men to Jesus. Look for the Southern Cross, and let it remind you of Christ's cross. Let your way through life be guided by the cross. It will keep you on course and bring you to a safe landing place with God.

> Jesus was born in the town of Bethlehem in Judaea, during the time when Herod was king. Soon afterwards, some men who studied the stars came from the east to Jerusalem and asked, 'Where is the baby born to be the king of the Jews? We saw his star when it came up in the east, and we have come to worship him.'
>
> When King Herod heard about this, he was very upset, and so was everyone else in Jerusalem. He called together all the chief priests and the teachers of the Law and asked them, 'Where will the Messiah be born?'
>
> 'In the town of Bethlehem in Judaea', they answered. 'For this is what the prophet wrote:

"Bethlehem in the land of Judah,
  you are by no means the least of the leading cities of
    Judah;
for from you will come a leader
  who will guide my people Israel" .'

So Herod called the visitors from the east to a secret meeting and found out from them the exact time the star had appeared. Then he sent them to Bethlehem, with these instructions: 'Go and make a careful search for the child, and when you find him, let me know, so that I too may go and worship him'.

And so they left, and on their way they saw the same star they had seen in the east. When they saw it, how happy they were, what joy was theirs! It went ahead of them until it stopped over the place where the child was. They went into the house, and when they saw the child with his mother Mary, they knelt down and worshipped him. They brought out their gifts of gold, frankincense, and myrrh, and presented them to him.

Then they returned to their country by another road, since God had warned them in a dream not to go back to Herod.

(Matthew 2:1–12 TEV)

The Chinese on the Australian Goldfields

The treatment of Chinese on Australian goldfields in the nineteenth century is one of the shameful episodes in our history.

The first Chinese were brought to Australia after the end of convict transportation to provide cheap labour for the colonies. But it was the gold rushes that brought big numbers of them to this country.

In China there was poverty and starvation at the time, and when news arrived of the discovery of gold in the big country to the south, many Chinese men were keen to go and try to better the lot of themselves and their families. In 1853 there were 2,000 Chinese in eastern Australia, but two years later, in 1855, there were 20,000. By 1861 the number had doubled to 40,000.

The Chinese were never liked by white Australians, and their presence on the goldfields was deeply resented. They were regarded with distrust and suspicion because of their different appearance, their different way of life, and their different religious beliefs and practices. One of the many accusations made against them was that they were carriers of loathsome diseases, including leprosy.

White resentment against them flared into mass violence on several occasions. One of the worst attacks occurred in 1857, when 100 white diggers clashed with 2,000 Chinese on the Buckland Valley diggings on the Ovens River in north-eastern Victoria. The whites resolved to expel the Chinese because of their 'gross and beastly practices', and because 'they were robbing us of our goldfields'. They bashed the Chinese with pick handles, robbed them of their gold and other possessions, and set fire to their camps. Several people were killed.

An even worse attack took place on June 30, 1861, at Lambing Flat, now the town of Young, New South Wales. Here a mob of about 2,000 white men attacked two groups of Chinese, one of about 300 and the other of about 500 people. There are eye-witness accounts of the brutality with which the Chinese were attacked, and the atrocities that took place. Again, several men were killed.

Some of the Chinese spent weeks after the attack hiding in the bush, with little clothing and no provisions, in bitterly cold winter weather. One local squatter, a man called James Robert, supplied food for several weeks to hundreds of these fugitive Chinamen.

A few of the men who took part in these attacks were later brought to trial, but anti-Chinese feeling was so strong that white juries refused to convict any of the accused.

Jesus was going into a village near the border between Samaria and Galilee, when he was met by ten men suffering from leprosy. Leprosy was the AIDS of Jesus' time. People were really frightened of it. Lepers were regarded as unclean, and were prohibited from taking part in religious services and ceremonies. They were excluded from everyday life and society. They were contaminated people, outcasts, the rejects of society.

In this group of ten lepers there was one who was a Samaritan. This made him an outcast in a double sense, because as a Samaritan he was hated and despised by the Jews.

The Samaritans were a mixed race, half Jew and half non-Jew, the result of intermarriage between Jews and Assyrian colonists who settled in the area after the conquest of the Northern Kingdom, Israel. The Jews hated the Samaritans because they were not racially pure and because they were not orthodox in their religious beliefs and practices. To a Jew, there was no one more repulsive and detestable than a Samaritan.

The ten lepers 'stood at a distance and shouted, "Jesus! Master! Take pity on us!" Jesus saw them and said to them, "Go and let the priests examine you". ' (Luke 17:12–14 TEV). (This was a legal requirement if one was to be pronounced free of the disease and so ritually clean.) As they were on their way, they found that they were healed of their leprosy.

One of the men, the Samaritan, when he saw that he was healed, came back, 'praising God in a loud voice. He threw himself to the ground at Jesus' feet and thanked him' (vv 15,16).

> Jesus said, 'There were ten men who were healed; where are the other nine? Why is this foreigner the only one who came back to give thanks to God?' And Jesus said to him, 'Get up and go; your faith has made you well' (vv 17–19).

The Samaritan was the only one who came back to say thank you, the only one who did the right thing.

He did this, he was more grateful than the others, because he was more of an outcast than the others. He was like a Chinaman on the Australian goldfields — a hated and despised foreigner, an outsider, an outcast. But this Jew, Jesus, had been good to him. He had helped him. He had shown compassion for him, and acceptance of him. He had healed him. He had shown that God's love and grace were for him too, the outcast, the foreigner. He had shown there was a place in God's kingdom also for him, the complete outsider.

We can imagine how thankful those Chinese hiding in the bush after the atrocities of Lambing Flat would have been for the help they received from James Robert. All their experiences with white people had been bad. But here was one white man who was prepared to risk his neck to help them. As Chinese, they would have been particularly grateful for this.

It was like that for the Samaritan. A kindness had been shown him which he could never have expected. That's why he came back praising God. That's why he threw himself at Jesus' feet to thank him.

We are like that Samaritan leper. In our relationship with God we are like Chinese on the Australian goldfields — we are foreigners, outcasts, complete outsiders. As sinners, as people infected with the AIDS virus of sin, we are unclean and have no place in God's kingdom.

And just as the Samaritan can't change himself into a Jew, or the Chinaman into a white man, so there is no way we can change ourselves from sinners into people who are acceptable to God.

But something has happened beyond all expectation. In Jesus, God has shown acceptance of us who were unacceptable. In Jesus he has touched us, the untouchables. He has heard the cry of the diseased and unclean. Through Christ and his cross, God has helped us in our need and made us whole. He has shown that there is a place in his kingdom also for us outcasts and outsiders.

When I see how God was not prejudiced against me even though I was quite different from him, this helps to break down my prejudice against people who are different from me. God's acceptance of me helps me to be more accepting of others. It helps me to hear the cries of those who are suffering, and gives me the courage to reach out and touch them.

We will never be thankful to God as long as we think that we are basically sound and good. We will never rejoice in God's goodness as long as we are proud of being a superior race, as long as we feel that we are God's own people who deserve something from him.

We are like Samaritans, like the Chinese. We are foreigners, outcasts, who can expect nothing from God. But in Jesus, he has been good to us beyond all expectation. That's why we praise him. That's why we can't stop thanking him.

> As Jesus made his way to Jerusalem, he went along the border between Samaria and Galilee. He was going into a village when he was met by ten men suffering from a dreaded skin-disease. They stood at a distance and shouted, 'Jesus! Master! Take pity on us!'
>
> Jesus saw them and said to them, 'Go and let the priests examine you'.
>
> On the way they were made clean.
>
> When one of them saw that he was healed, he came back, praising God in a loud voice. He threw himself to the ground at Jesus' feet and thanked him. The man was a Samaritan. Jesus said, 'There were ten men who were healed; where are the other nine? Why is this foreigner the only one who came back to give thanks to God?' And Jesus said to him, 'Get up and go; your faith has made you well'.
>
> (Luke 17:11–19 TEV)

The Queenstown Mine Disaster

One of Australia's worst mine disasters occurred in October 1912, in Queenstown on Tasmania's west coast. When fire broke out in the pump-house on the 700-foot level, 165 men were underground. Sixty-nine of them escaped, leaving 96 who were trapped.

The problem for the rescuers was that sections of the mine quickly filled with deadly carbon monoxide fumes. Over the next few days they kept testing the air in the mine by lowering chickens in cages at regular intervals, but whenever the chickens were brought up they were dead because of the poisoned air.

After several days, rescuers managed to find a way to break through to some of the trapped men, and 54 were eventually rescued. They were brought to the surface after spending four-and-a-half days in complete darkness and without food and water.

The remaining 42 men died because of the poisoned air. Their bodies were eventually found and brought to the surface.

We need to breathe clean air in order to stay alive. If the air we breathe becomes poisoned, we die.

The apostle John, in his First Letter, tells us that, as Christians, we need to test the spiritual air we are breathing to see whether it is clean or poisoned. He says: 'Dear friends, do not believe every spirit, but test the spirits to see whether they are from God, because many false prophets have gone out into the world' (1 John 4:1 NIV).

There are people around us with all kinds of values, attitudes, and ideas. There are many different organizations and religions, all with their own messages, their own beliefs and teachings. Some of these beliefs and teachings are like good, clean air — if you breathe this air you will stay alive. But other teachings are like poisoned air, and if you breathe this air you will die.

That's why John tells us to test the air we are breathing. He tells us to test the spirits, to test what we are hearing from others, to test the values and beliefs by which we are living. It's important for us to do this; in fact, it's a matter of life and death.

The people at the mine couldn't see or smell whether the air in the mine was fit to breathe or not. That's why they tested the air by lowering chickens down the mine.

What can we do to test the spiritual air that we are breathing? John tells us:

> This is how you can recognize the Spirit of God: Every spirit that acknowledges that Jesus Christ has come in the flesh is from God, but every spirit that does not acknowledge Jesus is not from God (vv 2,3).

It is what we say and believe about Jesus Christ that is the crucial test of whether the air we are breathing is pure or poisoned.

There were some people who had belonged to the Christian group to which John was writing, who claimed to have a superior, more enlightened understanding of the Christian message than other Christians. They denied that the Son of God had become a real human being of flesh and blood in the person of Jesus. They regarded it as absolutely impossible that God, who belongs to the spiritual realm and who is holy, could ever unite himself in this way with the material world, which they considered evil. So although they believed in a Christ, a Messiah, sent by God, it was not *Jesus* Christ, not the Christ who had become flesh in the person of Jesus of Nazareth.

To many people, this seemed an enlightened and attractive teaching. It seemed to protect the glory and honour of God by insisting that he had in no way been contaminated by direct contact with the material world.

But John says: 'No. This teaching is poison.'

> This is the spirit of the antichrist, which you have heard is coming and even now is already in the world ... They are from the world and therefore speak from the viewpoint of the world, and the world listens to them.

This teaching, John says, does not come from God and his Spirit. It comes from the enemy of Christ, the antichrist — it is anti-Christian. It comes from those who belong to the world, not those who belong to God.

If you follow this teaching, John says, if you breathe this polluted air, you will die.

The pure, clean air of the Gospel is quite different. The Gospel is the message that God did *not* avoid contact with us and our world in order to remain uncontaminated. Instead, he became one of us. In Jesus, he became a human being of flesh and blood like you and me, so that he could rescue us.

The miners who were trapped in the mine at Queenstown could not be helped by people staying above ground on the surface, hundreds of metres above them. If they were to be rescued, they needed people who could find ways of getting right down to where they were trapped. They needed fellow-miners who had the skill and the courage to reach them and bring them to the surface.

It was like that for us when we were trapped way down in the depths because of our sin, when we were in complete darkness, without food and drink, and breathing poisoned air. Unless someone could reach us and rescue us, we were going to die.

It was in Jesus that God found a way of breaking through to where we were trapped. In Jesus he became one of us, a fellow human being, a fellow-miner. He didn't stay up on the surface, far above us, and leave us to our fate. He found a way of reaching us. He came right down to where we were, right down into the mine, breathing our polluted air.

God became a human being of flesh and blood so that in Jesus he could give his life for us on the cross. It was on the cross that he showed his skill and courage in finding a way of reaching us. This is where he finally broke through to us. He found us. He rescued us. Through Jesus' death and resurrection he has brought us safely to the surface, out into the open, so that we can now breathe the clean, pure air of his forgiveness and his grace.

Keep testing the air you are breathing. Don't breathe polluted air. Don't let yourself be suffocated by false messages, false values and beliefs. Keep breathing deeply the pure air of the Gospel.

> *Dear friends, do not believe every spirit, but test the spirits to see whether they are from God, because many false prophets have gone out into the world. This is how you can recognize the Spirit of God: Every spirit that acknowledges that Jesus Christ has come in the flesh is from God, but every spirit that does not acknowledge Jesus is not from God. This is the spirit of the antichrist, which you have heard is coming and even now is already in the world.*

You, dear children, are from God and have overcome them, because the one who is in you is greater than the one who is in the world. They are from the world and therefore speak from the viewpoint of the world, and the world listens to them. We are from God, and whoever knows God listens to us; but whoever is not from God does not listen to us. This is how we recognize the Spirit of truth and the spirit of falsehood.

(1 John 4:1–6 NIV)

John McDouall Stuart and the Overland Telegraph Line

It was on October 25, 1861, that John McDouall Stuart left North Adelaide on his third attempt to find a way through central Australia to the north coast. The South Australian Government, keen for South Australia to be the first colony to establish a telegraph link with the rest of the world, had contributed £2,500 to help equip the expedition. Exactly nine months later, after tremendous difficulties and hardships, the party of ten men and 71 horses reached the coast, and Stuart was able to wash his face and hands in the waters of the Timor Sea.

His achievement opened the way for others to follow, and enabled important developments to take place. One of those who followed after him was Charles Todd, Postmaster General of South Australia. His great contribution was the construction of the Overland Telegraph Line between Adelaide and Darwin. The line linked up with a British underwater cable from Java to Darwin, and for the first time put the Australian colonies in telegraphic contact with the rest of the world.

The Overland Telegraph Line transformed certain aspects of life in Australia. It had taken Stuart nine months to travel the 3,500 km from Adelaide to Darwin. Now that distance could be covered, by means of the telegraph, in a matter of seconds. News from across the world that had taken weeks and months by ship was now received the following day. Commerce and trade were transformed, and Australia could now develop in new ways as a member of the international community.

Like Stuart, John the Baptist was out in the desert. There, in fulfilment of Old Testament prophecies, he was blazing a trail. He was preparing the way for someone else to follow. He was 'a voice of one calling in the desert, "Prepare the way for the Lord, make straight paths for him" ' (Mark 1:2 NIV).

John's appearance on the scene to prepare the way, to open up a track through the desert, means that big new developments are about to take place, exciting new possibilities are being opened up.

Original Post and Telegraph Office, Alice Springs, NT

Charles Todd, following behind Stuart, transformed life in Australia by constructing the Overland Telegraph Line. Jesus, following behind John along the way he had prepared for him, has transformed our life.

The coming of Jesus is like the establishing of a new communication link between us and God. He bridges that enormous distance between us and God, which we would never have been able to traverse ourselves. This is his great achievement. This is what makes his coming such an exciting event. We are no longer remote from God, no longer isolated from him. The coming of Jesus has brought us into direct and immediate contact with God.

In finding a track across the continent, Stuart had to confront and overcome tremendous difficulties. On occasions he had to find a way through rugged hills. At other times he had to find a way across great expanses of flat, waterless country, or through thick, dense scrub. These difficulties, together with the enormous distance, were like barriers blocking his way to the coast. His successful expedition prepared the way for the overcoming of the barriers, the conquest of the distance, through the construction of roads, railways, and the Overland Telegraph Line.

In a similar way, John's work prepared the way for the overcoming of the great distance and the barriers between us and God. The great barrier between us and God is sin. It's our own sinful human nature that cuts us off from God and keeps us separated and isolated from him.

This is why John, in preparing the way for Jesus, preaches that people should repent. The coming of Christ means that sin, that great barrier between us and God, is about to be confronted and overcome. That's why we are called to repent, to turn away from our sins. Repenting means wanting the barrier of my sin to be overcome, and it means looking to the one who is coming, to Jesus, to overcome this barrier for me.

The key to the overcoming of the distance between Adelaide and Darwin was water. Stuart on his expeditions was constantly preoccupied with finding water. Without sufficient water for men and horses, no progress could be made, the barriers couldn't be overcome. This is why the Telegraph Line, when it was constructed, followed places with names like Alice Springs, Barrow Creek, Tennant Creek, Newcastle Waters, Daly Waters. Without water the new communication links could not have been established.

Water is also the key to the overcoming of the distance and the barriers between us and God. John prepared the way for Jesus by baptizing people with water out in the desert. This baptism was for people who repented of their sin, so that they could receive God's forgiveness.

But John himself was quick to point out that the full and final overcoming of sin was still to come. The greater one, Jesus, who was coming after him, was bringing also a greater baptism. His baptism would still be baptism with water, but at the same time it would be a baptism with the Holy Spirit.

Before this baptism with the Spirit could be given, however, Jesus himself had to undergo another kind of baptism, a baptism of blood on the cross. It's through his death for us on the cross, and through his resurrection, that Jesus has gone out into the desert on our behalf and overcome the barrier of our sin.

In our own baptism, then, the Holy Spirit has united us with the crucified and risen Christ, so that his conquest of sin has become ours. It's in our baptism that Jesus became our Overland Telegraph Line, overcoming our isolation and separation from God. Here he himself became our direct and constant communication link with God.

And just as the Telegraph Line opened up new possibilities for the growth and development of this country, so our link with God through Jesus opens up new possibilities for us for growth and development. We are able to become more productive in what we can do for one another, in caring for each other, in breaking through the barriers that separate people from God and that separate us from each other.

The last section of the Overland Telegraph Line was finally joined on August 22, 1872. The first message along the newly-completed line was sent by Charles Todd. It read:

> We have this day, within two years, completed a line of communications 2,000 miles long through the very centre of Australia, until a few years ago a terra incognita believed to be a desert.

Celebratory banquets to mark the occasion were held in Adelaide, Sydney, and London.

We Christians have something even greater to celebrate. With the coming of Jesus, God has completed his line of communication between himself and us. This is the great event that has transformed our life and that we keep on celebrating.

> The beginning of the gospel about Jesus Christ, the Son of God.
> It is written in Isaiah the prophet:
> 'I will send my messenger ahead of you,
> who will prepare your way' —
> 'a voice of one calling in the desert,
> "Prepare the way for the Lord,
> make straight paths for him". '
> And so John came, baptizing in the desert region and preaching repentance and baptism for the forgiveness of sins. The whole Judean countryside and all the people of Jerusalem went out to him. Confessing their sins, they were baptized by him in the Jordan River. John wore clothing made of camel's hair, with a leather belt around his waist, and he ate locusts and wild honey. And this was his message: 'After me will come one more powerful than I, the thongs of whose sandals I am not worthy to stoop down and untie. I baptize you with water, but he will baptize you with the Holy Spirit.'
>
> (Mark 1:1–8 NIV)

Drought Conditions in the Mallee

My father began his work as a pastor in the mallee country of South Austrlia, first at Pinnaroo, and then at Loxton, where I was born. He has sometimes spoken about the terrible droughts that occurred there in the 1930s and '40s, when choking dust storms were common, and drift-sand buried roads, railway lines, and fences.

I remember him speaking on one occasion about a newspaper reporter who came up-country to have a look at conditions first-hand. In his subsequent article in the paper he wrote: 'This is the end. This country will never recover.' The reporter was appalled by what he had seen. The situation appeared hopeless. The desolation seemed complete, and a future for the land seemed non-existent.

This is how the people of Israel felt when they were in exile in Babylon. They had suffered a terrible catastrophe: the complete destruction of their city and the loss of their land. They felt that as a people they were finished. They could see no future for themselves. This was the end. This was something from which they could never recover.

It was at this time that the prophet Ezekiel was given a vision by God. He was taken by the spirit of the Lord and set down in a valley where the ground was covered with human bones. It was a scene of utter desolation and death.

Ezekiel noticed that the bones were very dry — these people had been dead a long time. God asked him: 'Mortal man, can these bones come back to life?' Ezekiel replied: 'Sovereign Lord, only you can answer that!' (Ezek. 37:3 TEV). But of course the answer was obvious — these dead people, of whom only the dry bones were left, could never come to life again.

These dry bones represented the people of Israel. Later on God said to Ezekiel: 'The people of Israel are like these bones. They say that they are dried up, without any hope and with no future' (v 11).

But God had a message for these dry bones. He told Ezekiel to speak to them: 'Tell these dry bones to listen to the word of the Lord'. Ezekiel was to give them this promise from God: 'I will give you sinews and muscles, and cover you with skin. I will put breath

Effects of drought

into you and bring you back to life. Then you will know that I am the Lord' (vv 4,6).

Ezekiel did what he was told — he spoke God's message to the bones. And an amazing thing happened. Ezekiel saw all the bones coming together and then being covered with sinews, muscles, flesh, and skin. Then, at God's command, he spoke to the wind, and the wind came and put breath into the lifeless bodies, and they came alive and stood up, an army of living people.

God's message for his people through this vision was that he would make the impossible happen for them. He was going to bring them back to life. He had a future mapped out for them. He would rescue them. He would give them new life as a nation, and new hope.

It was going to be such a transformation of their fortunes that it would be like a resurrection from the dead. It would be like a new act of creation. There was hope for them after all. This was not the end. Recovery was possible. Just as drought-stricken land bursts into life again with the coming of rain, so this dead and defeated people would be raised up again to new life.

Times of drought and barrenness occur in our life, times when the joy goes out of life, and everything is bleak and wretched. These are the times when there seems to be nothing to look forward to. I may be battling with sickness or pain, or facing death. There may be conflict with other people, or the distress of a broken relationship. There may simply be the worries and pressures, the tensions and anxieties, of life. Or there may be the shock of an accident causing the death of someone close to me. There may also be the shame of something careless or stupid I did in the past, some terrible mistake that I am now going to have to live with for the rest of my life.

There are times when I look over the bare and barren paddocks of my life and say to myself: 'This country will never recover'. I feel that there are things here I can never escape. All I can see are the dry bones of fear, failure, and death.

But in Ezekiel's vision God gives us the same promise that he gave his people in exile. He promises rain for the drought-stricken paddocks of our life. He promises to transform our situation. There is hope of a recovery. We are not condemned to carry for ever into the future the burden of our past, with all its silly mistakes. God promises us new life, new hope, a new future.

This new life comes to us through God's powerful and creative Word. The dry bones became living human beings when Ezekiel spoke God's word of promise to them. It's when we hear God speaking to us that our life is renewed and restored.

God's supreme word of promise has been spoken to us in Jesus, the Word that became flesh. It's through his death and resurrection that God brings us back to life. This is where he gives us new life, new hope, and a new future. He comes to us here like rain on dry ground, bringing to an end the barrenness and desolation caused by sin and death.

'Listen to the word of the Lord.' This is the message for us when we look to our guilty past. This is the message for us when we look to a bleak and uncertain future. To listen to the Word of the Lord means listening to the promise that God gives us through Jesus and his death and resurrection. The promise is that the God who raised his Son Jesus from death will also raise us to life.

Our life may be drought-stricken — desolate and dry. The future may look hopeless. But the promise of God is that this is not the end. The country will recover. Because of Christ, the bare and barren land will bloom again, the dry bones will be brought back to life.

I felt the powerful presence of the Lord, and his spirit took me and set me down in a valley where the ground was covered with bones. He led me all round the valley, and I could see that there were very many bones and that they were very dry. He said to me, 'Mortal man, can these bones come back to life?'

I replied, 'Sovereign Lord, only you can answer that!'

He said, 'Prophesy to the bones. Tell these dry bones to listen to the word of the Lord. Tell them that I, the Sovereign Lord, am saying to them: I am going to put breath into you and bring you back to life. I will give you sinews and muscles, and cover you with skin. I will put breath into you and bring you back to life. Then you will know that I am the Lord.'

So I prophesied as I had been told. While I was speaking, I heard a rattling noise, and the bones began to join together. While I watched, the bones were covered with sinews and muscles, and then with skin. But there was no breath in the bodies.

God said to me, 'Mortal man, prophesy to the wind. Tell the wind that the Sovereign Lord commands it to come from every direction, to breathe into these dead bodies, and to bring them back to life.'

So I prophesied as I had been told. Breath entered the bodies, and they came to life and stood up. There were enough of them to form an army.

God said to me, 'Mortal man, the people of Israel are like these bones. They say that they are dried up, without any hope and with no future. So prophesy to my people Israel and tell them that I, the Sovereign Lord, am going to open their graves. I am going to take them out and bring them back to the land of Israel. When I open the graves where my people are buried and bring them out, they will know that I am the Lord. I will put my breath in them, bring them back to life, and let them live in their own land. Then they will know that I am the Lord. I have promised that I would do this — and I will. I, the Lord, have spoken.'

(Ezekiel 37:1–14 TEV)

Our Olympic Gold Medallists

'Five metres, four, three, two, one — Gold! Gold to Australia! Gold! Gold! Gold!'

It was the ABC's Norman May at the 1980 Moscow Olympic Games. The event was the swimming 4 x 100 metres medley relay, and the team of Mark Kerry, Peter Evans, Mark Tonelli, and Neil Brooks had just won Australia's first Olympic gold medal since Munich in 1972.

In many sports, it's the greatest prize you can win — an Olympic gold medal. Athletes often value it more than a world record — records can be beaten, but no one can take away an Olympic gold medal. It means that, at that particular time, you were the best in the world.

Olympic gold medals don't come easily. To have any chance of winning, you first have to gain selection in the Olympic team. To get selected, you have to qualify, and to qualify, you have to be good. To achieve the required level, you not only need the natural ability but you have to have done hours and hours of hard training. Only a few are good enough to qualify and gain selection, and of these only the very top athlete will go on to win an Olympic gold medal.

In his second letter to Timothy, St Paul speaks of himself winning a trophy. At the time of writing he was in prison because of his faith in Christ, and he knew that he could be executed at any time. That's why he begins by saying: 'I am already being poured out like a drink offering, and the time has come for my departure' (2 Tim. 4:6 NIV).

He pictures his life as a Christian as being like an athletic contest, a race. Not only has he managed to finish the race, but he has won — he has taken the gold medal.

> I have fought the good fight, I have finished the race, I have kept the faith. Now there is in store for me the crown of righteousness, which the Lord, the righteous Judge, will award to me on that day — and not only to me, but also to all who have longed for his appearing. (2 Timothy 4:7,8 NIV).

Only the very top athletes are good enough to win an Olympic gold medal. What about the greatest award of all, the crown of righteousness, the prize of eternal life? How hard is it to win this

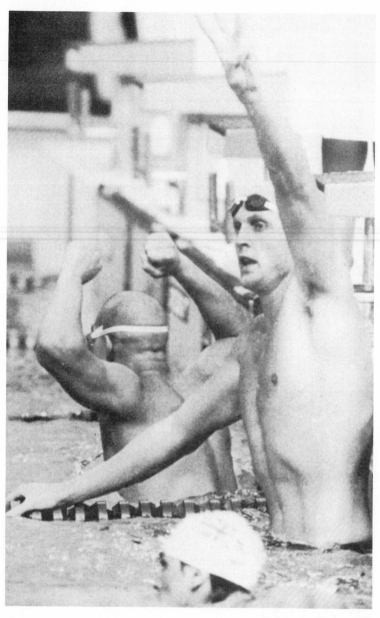

Neil Brooks, Moscow, 1980

prize? It must be tough to qualify. You'd have to be good. Only very few of the very best would make it.

The truth is that *nobody* makes it. Nobody is good enough. Nobody qualifies.

As far as meeting God's qualifying standard is concerned, we're not only like athletes who just aren't good enough, but it's as if we are carrying a serious injury or have a serious disability. This is what the Bible calls sin.

Sin is not just an occasional wrong thing we do. Instead, it is like a chronic injury, or a permanent disability. And just as a bad injury keeps us from competing and gives us no hope of winning gold, so sin keeps us out of the race, it disqualifies us from a life lived in fellowship with God. It makes the crown of righteousness — eternal life — an impossible dream. It leads to that worst of all deaths — permanent separation from God.

Nothing we can do could ever get us out of this situation. There is no way we can get ourselves fit, no way we could ever get into the race or become good enough to qualify.

But in Jesus God has come to our help. He has sent Jesus as the expert in dealing with our injury, our disability. Jesus has the ability to cure us of the crippling effects of sin.

He has done this for us in his death on the cross. This was the great race that he ran, the terrific contest in which he himself took part. This is where he took on the opposition, God's great opponents — sin, death, and the devil — and won. It looked as if they'd beaten him. But when God raised him to life again, it became clear that he was the winner.

This great victory that Jesus won on the cross can become our victory. This happens when we become part of his team, when we put ourselves in his hands and let him become our team doctor and coach. He's the one who can deal with our injuries and disabilities. He's the one who can forgive our sin. Because of him, we can qualify and gain selection in God's team. He's the brilliant coach who can outwit the opposition and get the gold medal for us.

What's required on our part is simply that we put ourselves in the coach's hands, that we trust him, that we believe in him, that we listen to him and follow what he says. We need to remember that without him we've got no hope — we wouldn't even be in the race. It's only with him that we can get to stand on the winner's podium and have that gold medal put around our neck.

And once he's got us in the race, once he's got us out there on the track, the important thing is to give it everything we've got, to keep going and not give up, to make sure that we don't throw away the opportunity he's given us. We need to keep going till we cross the finish line, till the end of the race, till the day we die. This simply means living our whole life relying on Jesus, and not losing our faith and trust in him. This is what St Paul means when he says: 'I have fought the good fight, I have finished the race, I have kept the faith'.

St Paul had not only kept on holding to the faith himself, but he had also worked hard to make the Christian faith known to others. He was like a champion athlete who devotes time to coaching younger competitors and passing on to them his knowledge and experience. He wants many others to enjoy the same success that he has had, and to win the same prize that he has won because of Jesus.

We should be doing the same. We who have already won our gold medal need to share our knowledge and experience with others, so that they can be winners too.

St Paul wrote these words when he was facing death. He was soon going to be executed because of his Christian faith. But although he was soon going to die, we see no sign of fear or distress or bitterness. Instead, we hear him speaking with confident trust and complete assurance.

He can do this because he already knows the outcome of the contest that lies ahead. He knows that the gold medal is his — he's got a mortgage on it. He knows that it's his because he has Jesus. He knows that Jesus has already won gold for him.

It's because of Jesus that we can face death with the same courage and confidence. The gold medal is already ours. We are already involved in the victory celebrations.

Jesus is the greatest winner of all time. Together with him, we can be winners too.

Captain Cook and Possession Island

Do not be afraid — I will save you.
I have called you by name — you are
mine.
(Isaiah 43:1 TEV)

In 1769, after observing the transit of Venus across the sun, Captain James Cook left Tahiti and sailed south in the *Endeavour* in search of 'the Great South Land'. He discovered New Zealand and explored its coast, and then landed on the coast of New Holland on April 29, 1770, at a place he called Botany Bay.

From there he sailed up the coast, almost coming to grief on the Great Barrier Reef, to the tip of Cape York Peninsula. There, on August 22, 1770, on a small island to which he gave the name Possession Island, he 'hoisted English colours' and took possession of the eastern coast of New Holland in the name of King George III. He named the land New South Wales.

Captain Cook was not the first European sailor to visit the shores of this country. But his achievement was to secure the land for the British, and it was this action which led to the sailing of the First Fleet 18 years later and the establishing of the convict settlement at Sydney Cove in January 1788.

For Cook, as for other Europeans at that time, the lands discovered were new lands; that's why the word 'new' occurs so often in the names given to these countries — New Holland, New Zealand, New South Wales. What happened eventually, of course, was that new nations came into existence in these lands, with new populations made up of settlers from many different countries, together with the original inhabitants.

What James Cook did in taking possession of this land for the British king is similar to what God has done for us through Christ. Jesus was sent to this earth in order to take possession of it. He came to claim the world for God, for the King. He did this so that God's rule, God's kingdom, could be established here on earth.

His coming to earth was his great voyage of discovery. It was a journey which took him to the cross, into the great unknown regions of death and hell.

But it was a successful voyage. There on the cross he discovered you and me and took possession of us, claiming us for God.

This has happened for each of us individually in our baptism. This is where Jesus called me by name and I became his. This is where he came and claimed me for God, taking possession of me so that I could come under God's saving rule in his kingdom.

And just as Captain Cook's action led to the emergence of a new people, a new nation, so Jesus' work also has brought into existence a new nation, a new people. This is the new people of God, which is called God's church. This new nation is made up of people from all over the world who belong to Christ, just as our own nation of Australia has been formed by people coming here from many different countries.

We are Australian Christians — Australians who are also part of God's commonwealth, Christians who are also members of the Commonwealth of Australia.

We are proud to be Australians, happy to belong to this country. On our national holidays, Australia Day and Anzac Day, we remember our past and celebrate our achievements as a nation. We can be thankful that we can live in this good land and be part of this nation.

At the same time, we are proud to be Christians, happy to belong to the new people of God. On our great holy days we remember and celebrate the great things God has done for us through Christ, and the things we've been able to achieve because of his goodness to us. We are thankful that we can live in God's good land, the church, as members of his commonwealth.

As you think of your identity as an Australian Christian, remember the initials J.C. Remember James Cook, who took possession of this land for the English king and paved the way for the formation of this new nation to which we now belong. And remember Jesus Christ, who on the cross took possession of us for God, so that we can now live as God's new people under his rule in his kingdom.

But there are also responsibilities and tasks that face us as Australian Christians. Our past has not always been glorious. As a nation and as a church we have also failed and made mistakes. Given our past and what we are today, what is our task for the future?

We cannot live in a selfish and self-centred way as individuals or as a nation. The danger is that we remain preoccupied with our own standard of living and become indifferent, unconcerned,

Tropical beach scene, Qld

and uncaring about people who are suffering and in need. How fair-dinkum are we about our claim to be people who give everyone a fair go?

We need to be involved in organizations that make a contribution to our community and nation, and that try to do something constructive about the critical questions facing our world today.

At the same time, as Australian Christians, we need to be actively involved in the task that God has given us to find ways of making the Good News of Jesus known in our communities. We need to do this so that Jesus can keep on taking possession of new territory, claiming also our fellow-Australians for God, so that they can come under his saving rule in his kingdom.

What we need in all of this is to catch something of the spirit of a Captain Cook — to be prepared to sail into unknown waters, to face difficulties and dangers with courage, to be ready to attempt something new and to make new discoveries; and all of this so that our country, our nation, can be taken possession of by Christ, can be claimed for God.

Captain James Cook is one of the great names in our history. But for us the greatest of all names is the name of Jesus. His name is great because of his great voyage of discovery to the cross, where he found you and me and took possession of us for God.

Now we can make his name even greater by making him known to our fellow Australians, so that they can be claimed for God too, and can join us as members of God's new nation.

Tragedy on Lake Alexandrina

My wife's parents live in the small town of Milang on the shore of Lake Alexandrina, the large freshwater lake at the mouth of the Murray River in South Australia. We like visiting their place with its lovely view over the broad expanses of the lake.

At most times, the lake seems very placid. But when the storms come in off the Southern Ocean, the shallow waters get whipped up into short, steep waves, and it becomes a wild and treacherous place, where many people have lost their lives over the years.

It was late Saturday afternoon on August 22, 1987, that a group of Scouts were paddling their canoes across a shorter stretch of water between islands at the western end of the lake, when a violent storm struck with savage suddenness. Within minutes, powerless against the force of the wind and the waves, they were swept out into the body of the lake. Four of them were drowned.

Others would almost certainly have died of exposure during the night except for one of the marvels of modern technology. Four of them were found at midnight, huddled together in reed-beds on the other side of the lake, by an RAAF helicopter whose crewmen were using special goggles that enabled them to see in the dark. Because of the extremely poor visibility there was no way that they would otherwise have been spotted, and by next morning it would probably have been too late.

On Lake Galilee the disciples of Jesus also experienced a miraculous rescue. They had set out in the evening to sail across the lake, but had got into trouble when they were hit by a violent storm. All night they had battled the wind and the waves, and in the early hours of the morning, drenched and cold, in pitch darkness, with the storm still raging, they were near the end of their strength.

It was just then that help came, and they were rescued. It came against all hope and expectation, in the middle of the night, at the height of the storm. The impossible happened. Jesus came to them, walking through the storm, walking on the water through the wild crashing waves.

At first they were terrified. With all the devils of the storm screaming around them and clutching at them, they thought that here was the ghost come to claim their lives. But then they heard

Aerial view of Lake Alexandrina and the Murray mouth

a voice, and the sound of that voice changed everything: 'Courage! It is I. Don't be afraid!' (Matt. 14:27 TEV).

They recognized it as the voice of Jesus. Miraculously, help had come. They realized that they were rescued. Jesus was with them. They knew that they were safe.

Jesus was not the first to walk on water. Parts of the Old Testament speak of God walking on the waters of the ocean: 'When the waters saw you, O God, they were afraid, and the depths of the sea trembled... You walked through the waves; you crossed the deep sea, but your footprints could not be seen' (Ps. 77:16,19 TEV).

The people of Israel were afraid of the sea; for them it was a symbol of all powerful destructive forces, all the evil powers that bring distress, destruction, and death. When God walks on the water it means that he is showing his mastery over the sea, his power over wind and wave, over all the evil forces in this world that can destroy us. 'It is his strength that conquered the sea' (Job 26:12).

This is what makes Jesus' walking on the water so exciting. Here is someone who is a human being like you and me, but who has God's own power over the wind and the waves.

He didn't walk on smooth water, but on wild, raging water, water threatening to swamp the boat and drown the disciples. He walks on this dangerous, treacherous water, and in doing this he shows his mastery over it, his contempt for it. He shows that he has power to trample under foot, to walk all over, all the things that have power to hurt us and destroy us.

When Jesus had got into the boat and the wind had died down, the disciples worshipped him, saying: 'Truly you are the Son of God!' (Matt. 14:33). There on the lake they had seen that God himself and his power were present in this man.

It was later, at the foot of the cross, that these words were spoken again. When the army officer and the soldiers who had carried out Jesus' execution saw what happened in connection with his death, they exclaimed: 'He really was the Son of God!' (Matt. 27:54 TEV). There at the cross they had seen that God and his power were present in this man.

It's on the cross that Jesus has trampled on all the things that can hurt us. This is where he trod under foot the wind and the waves. Here he walked all over sin and death and the devil, showing his mastery over them and destroying their power to harm us.

When the squall suddenly hits, when we find ourselves swept into the middle of the lake, powerless against the force of the wind and the waves, Jesus comes to our rescue. In the middle of the night, at the height of the storm, suddenly he is there with us.

He is not present as a ghost, but as the one who became flesh and blood for us, and who bled and died for us on the cross. In the bread and wine of Holy Communion, he comes to us when we are weak and helpless, frightened and exhausted, and he says to us: 'Courage! It is I. I'm here for you. Don't be afraid!'

When the disciples realized that it was Jesus who was coming to them on the water, Peter said: 'Lord, if it is really you, order me to come out on the water to you' (Matt. 14:28). Jesus told him to come. So Peter got out of the boat and started walking on the water to Jesus.

What Peter did was impossible. Nobody can defy wind and waves in that way. But Peter did it, not because of himself and his own ability, but because of Jesus and his power. The amazing thing is that Jesus gives to those who trust him his own mastery over the wind and the waves, his own victory over evil and death.

But in the darkness and the storm it's not easy to believe. Peter got scared when he saw how strong the wind was, and he started to sink. He cried out: 'Save me, Lord!' At once Jesus reached out and grabbed hold of him and said, 'How little faith you have! Why did you doubt?' (vv 30,31).

There are times when we get scared, times when our faith is shaken, times when we are filled with doubt. Peter, the boldest of Jesus' disciples, was not immune from such fears and such doubts. Later on, his faith failed again when he desperately denied that he had ever known Jesus.

Not even the one with the strongest faith among us can rely on his or her faith. We are always people of too little faith.

But we *can* rely on Jesus, and this is where we need to keep our eyes fixed. He's the one we can trust. We will fail, we will fall. But when we cry out to him, as Peter did, 'Save me, Lord!', he is always right there to grab hold of us and lift us up again.

Don't be frightened of the wind and the waves. Jesus is there with you in the darkness and in the storm. On the cross he has walked all over everything that can hurt you. Trust him, and you'll be able to walk on top of the waves too.

> Then Jesus made the disciples get into the boat and go on ahead to the other side of the lake, while he sent the people away. After sending the people away, he went up a hill by himself to pray. When evening came, Jesus was there alone; and by this time the boat was far out in the lake, tossed about by the waves, because the wind was blowing against it.
>
> Between three and six o'clock in the morning Jesus came to the disciples, walking on the water. When they saw him walking on the water, they were terrified. 'It's a ghost!' they said, and screamed with fear.
>
> Jesus spoke to them at once. 'Courage!' he said. 'It is I. Don't be afraid!'
>
> Then Peter spoke up. 'Lord, if it is really you, order me to come out on the water to you'.
>
> 'Come!' answered Jesus. So Peter got out of the boat and started walking on the water to Jesus. But when he noticed the strong wind, he was afraid and started to sink down in the water. 'Save me, Lord!' he cried.
>
> At once Jesus reached out and grabbed hold of him and said, 'How little faith you have! Why did you doubt?'
>
> They both got into the boat, and the wind died down. Then the disciples in the boat worshipped Jesus. 'Truly you are the Son of God!' they exclaimed.
>
> (Matthew 14:22–33 TEV)

Edward John Eyre and the Aboriginal Guide

It was on June 18, 1840, that the exploration party led by Edward John Eyre was given an official farewell at Government House on North Terrace, Adelaide. The party then rode down the hill, crossed the bridge over the River Torrens, galloped through North Adelaide, and headed north. The aim of the expedition was to penetrate to the centre of the continent and, if possible, carry on right through to the north coast.

They didn't succeed. At the end of the Flinders Ranges they found their way barred by huge salt lakes (one of which now bears Eyre's name) and were unable to find a way through.

Reluctant to return to Adelaide admitting defeat, Eyre travelled down the west side of Spencer Gulf, on the west-coast peninsula that also bears his name. At Fowler's Bay he decided to attempt a crossing of the continent to the west, around the Great Australian Bight. He took with him one white companion, Baxter, and three Aborigines — Joey and Yarry from New South Wales, and Wylie from Albany in Western Australia.

Halfway along the journey, Baxter was killed and Joey and Yarry ran away. It was left to Eyre and Wylie to carry on alone. Just over a year after leaving Adelaide, they staggered into the small settlement at Albany to bring to an end the most terrible and incredible journey on foot by any Australian explorers.

Eyre was the first to acknowledge that he would never have accomplished this great feat if it hadn't been for help he'd received from Aborigines. In all those hundreds of kilometres between Fowler's Bay and Albany, there were only two or three places where water could be found, by digging for it in the sandhills. At the head of the Bight, friendly Aborigines told Eyre about these places and how to find them. Without this information, he would have wasted an enormous amount of time and effort looking for water where there was none, and he could easily have walked straight past the few places where it could be found. He also benefited from the bushcraft of the Aborigines travelling with him. On some of the long waterless stretches they showed him how to get a little water by digging up tree roots and cutting off the ends to let the water drain out.

Eyre was not the only explorer who owed his survival in the desert to Aborigines. At that time, white people considered themselves superior in every way to the Aborigines. The

Witjina of Areyonga, NT

Aborigines were looked down on and treated as inferiors. The white man was always boss, always the one in authority.

But occasionally, in certain life-and-death situations, the roles were reversed. When it came to a matter of survival in the desert, it became clear that the Aborigine was the expert. In this area he was the authority.

There was a Roman officer who turned to Jesus for help. He had a servant, very dear to him, who was sick and about to die. He sent some Jewish elders to Jesus to ask him to come and heal his servant.

For this man to turn to Jesus for help was like a white explorer turning for help to an Aborigine. The Romans ruled the world at that time, just as Britain ruled the waves last century. And just as the Europeans looked down on the Aborigines, the Romans looked down on other races and nationalities. As far as the Romans were concerned, the Jews were a small, weak, insignificant people of no importance at all. What Roman would ever turn to a Jew for help?

But that's what this Roman officer does. He does it because he's faced with a life-and-death situation in which he's helpless. He's a powerful man, used to wielding authority. 'I, too', he says, 'am a man placed under the authority of superior officers, and I have soldiers under me. I order this one "Go!" and he goes; I order that one "Come!" and he comes; and I order my slave, "Do this!" and he does it' (Luke 7:8 TEV). But in the face of death his authority ends.

That's why he comes to Jesus. He has heard of him, and somehow he has come to the conviction that in the face of sickness and death this Jew is the expert. 'Just give the order', he says, 'and my servant will get well' (v 7). He acknowledges that in this situation, where it's a question of survival, Jesus is the authority.

His confidence is not misplaced. Jesus shows that he does have authority in this area. He knows how to ensure survival in the face of sickness and death. With almost nonchalant ease, without even going to see the man, he heals him.

We can imagine that the explorer, realizing that his survival in the desert now depends on these Aborigines, might suddenly feel bad about his previous attitude and behaviour toward them. He has always looked down on them and treated them as inferiors. Now they are caring for him, and he depends on them for survival. He might well feel ashamed and say to himself: 'Why should these people help me? As far as they're concerned I'm an invader, taking their land and disrupting their life. They owe me nothing. I deserve nothing from them. They would be justified in regarding me as an enemy and leaving me to perish.'

All of us who have come to know Jesus and what he's done to rescue us feel like this. We feel unworthy. We realize that we are people who have wronged God. Our attitude and our behaviour toward him have not been right. We deserve nothing from him. He owes me nothing. He would be justified in treating me as an enemy and leaving me to perish.

This is how this Roman officer feels. He's actually a good man. The Jewish authorities speak well of him to Jesus: 'This man really deserves your help. He loves our people and he himself built a synagogue for us' (Luke 7:4,5). But in his message to Jesus he says nothing about this himself. He doesn't brag about his good works in order to persuade Jesus to help him. Instead, he speaks of his unworthiness. Having asked Jesus to come and help, he then sends some friends to say: 'Sir, don't trouble yourself. I do not deserve to have you come into my house, neither do I consider myself worthy to come to you in person' (vv 6,7).

None of us has deserved what Jesus has done for us. None of us is worthy of his rescue of us. Just as Aborigines were sometimes kinder to white explorers than they deserved, so God is kinder to us than we deserve. Through Jesus' death and resurrection God has rescued us in spite of our unworthiness. His rescue of us is an act of complete undeserved kindness, an act of sheer grace.

When the explorer is facing death in the desert and only the Aborigines can save him, the only thing for him to do is put himself in their hands. He has to trust them, he has to put his faith in them. Nothing else that he's prided himself on previously will help him — his ancestry, his race, his nationality, his education, his wealth. He must simply entrust himself to the Aborigines. He must believe them when they say that they can lead him to water. When they put stuff in his hands that doesn't look fit for human consumption, he must believe that it's good food which will keep him alive.

That's what this Roman officer did — he simply believed that Jesus could and would help him. That's what Jesus commended him for — not for his goodness, but for his faith. 'I tell you', he said, ' I have never found faith like this, not even in Israel!' (Luke 7:9).

That's all Jesus wants from us. He wants us to trust him. He wants us to believe that he can rescue us. He wants us to have faith in his power and authority in the face of death.

Life can be like a desert for us, a hard and harsh place where we face distress and danger and death. Jesus is the Aboriginal guide sent to us by God to guide us safely through this desert. He is the one who was despised and rejected, but who turned out to be our saviour. He's the authority on how to survive in the desert. He knows the desert like the back of his hand. Through his death and resurrection he has overcome all the dangers for us. We can trust him. We can confidently entrust ourselves to him.

> When Jesus had finished saying all these things to the people, he went to Capernaum. A Roman officer there had a servant who was very dear to him; the man was sick and about to die. When the officer heard about Jesus, he sent some Jewish elders to ask him to come and heal his servant. They came to Jesus and begged him earnestly, 'This man really deserves your help. He loves our people and he himself built a synagogue for us.'
>
> So Jesus went with them. He was not far from the house when the officer sent friends to tell him, 'Sir, don't trouble yourself. I do not deserve to have you come into my house, neither do I consider myself worthy to come to you in person. Just give the order, and my servant will get well. I, too, am a man placed under the authority of superior officers, and I have soldiers under me. I order this one, "Go!" and he goes; I order that one, "Come!" and he comes; and I order my slave, "Do this!" and he does it.'
>
> Jesus was surprised when he heard this; he turned round and said to the crowd following him, 'I tell you, I have never found faith like this, not even in Israel!'
>
> The messengers went back to the officer's house and found his servant well.
>
> (Luke 7:1–10 TEV)

Photo Credits

Cover
   King's Canyon, NT — Peter Thamm
Page
   5 Approaching Brachina, Flinders Ranges, SA — Helen Schubert
   8 Royal Flying Doctor Service aeroplane — Royal Flying Doctor Service of Australia
  25 Lighthouse at Port Adelaide, SA — SA State Promotion Unit
  27 Aboriginal waterhole, Kanyaka, SA — SA State Promotion Unit
  43 'Simpson and his donkey', sculpture by Peter Corlett — Australian War Memorial, Canberra, photo by Peter West
  47 Football barrackers — *The Advertiser*
  50 After Ash Wednesday bu....... — *The Advertiser*
  56 Fleurieu Coast, SA — SA Department of Tourism
  63 Sunrise — Jeff Sawade
  69 Sovereign Hill, Vic. — P. Munchenberg
  71 Ayers Rock, NT — John Pfitzner
  80 The Strehlow family and Aboriginal friends, Hermannsburg, NT, about 1917 — from *Aborigines, Artefacts and Anguish*
  93 Statue of Catherine Helen Spence, Light Square, Adelaide, SA — Graeme Cogdell
  96 Cyclone Tracy devastation, Darwin, NT — G. Simpson
 100 Zealous gold diggers, 1852, by S.T. Gill — La Trobe Collection, State Library of Victoria
 110 On an outback road — Norm Hamdorf
 119 Black snake — SA State Promotion Unit
 125 Replica of the 'Southern Cross' — *The Advertiser*
 138 Original Post and Telegraph Office, Alice Springs, NT — John Pfitzner
 142 Effects of drought — *The Advertiser*
 146 Neil Brooks, Moscow, 1980 — Olympic Council of NSW
 151 Tropical beach scene, Qld — John Hoopmann
 153 Aerial view of Lake Alexandrina and the Murray mouth — John Hoopmann
 157 Witjina of Areyonga, NT — from *Hermannsburg: A Vision and a Mission*